D0515176

*Visual Factfinder*

# COUNTRIES
## OF THE
# WORLD

*Visual Factfinder*

# COUNTRIES
# OF THE
# WORLD

BRIAN WILLIAMS

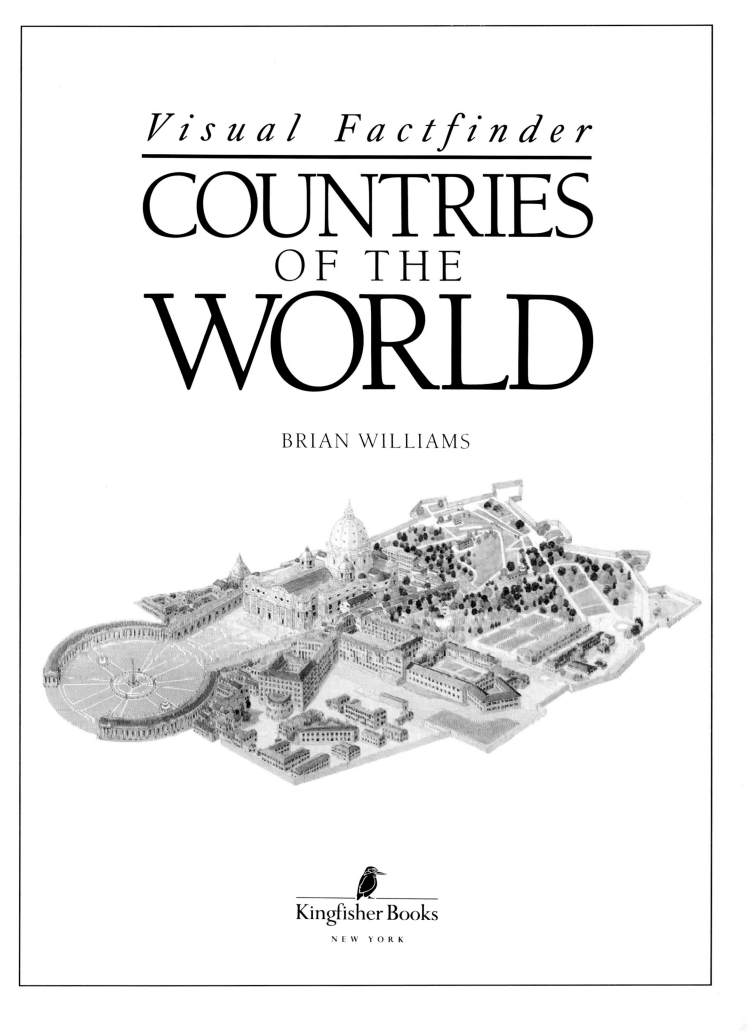

Kingfisher Books

NEW YORK

KINGFISHER BOOKS
Grisewood & Dempsey Inc.
95 Madison Avenue
New York, New York 10016

First American edition 1993
2 4 6 8 10 9 7 5 3 1 (lib. bdg.)
2 4 6 8 10 9 7 5 3 1 (pbk.)

Copyright © Grisewood & Dempsey Ltd. 1993

All rights reserved under International and Pan-American Copyright Conventions

Library of Congress Cataloging-in-Publication Data
Williams, Brian
Countries of the world: a visual factfinder/Brian Williams.—
1st American ed.
p.    cm.—(Visual factfinders)
Includes index.
Summary: Charts, diagrams, illustrations, maps, and text present
facts and figures about the countries and peoples of today's world.
1. Geography—Juvenile literature.    [1. Geography.]    I. Title.
II. Series.
G133.W55    1993
910—dc20          92-40367    CIP    AC

ISBN 1-85697-844-3 (lib. bdg.)
ISBN 1-85697-816-8 (pbk.)

Series Editor: Michèle Byam
Assistant Editor: Cynthia O'Neill
Series Designer: Ralph Pitchford
Design Assistant: Sandra Begnor
Picture Research: Su Alexander

Additional help from Nicky Barber, Catherine Bradley,
Andy Archer, Janet Woronkowicz, Hilary Bird

Printed in Spain

# CONTENTS

# About this Factfinder

This encyclopedic reference book gives essential facts and figures about the continents, the countries of each continent, and the cultures and lifestyles of the peoples who live in those countries. Each topic is interpreted in a highly visual style with color illustrations, maps, diagrams, and photographs that complement the text.

Political maps show the position of the world's independent countries, and give up-to-date facts on population, language, economics, and healthcare.

Short text essays introduce each of the continents, as well as the more specialized topics of the world's cultures, and its economic and political systems.

Detailed illustrations show scenes and objects that give an idea of the great diversity of cultures and lifestyles of people throughout the world.

Extra information on countries' religions, languages, customs, products, and health and government systems is given in fact boxes.

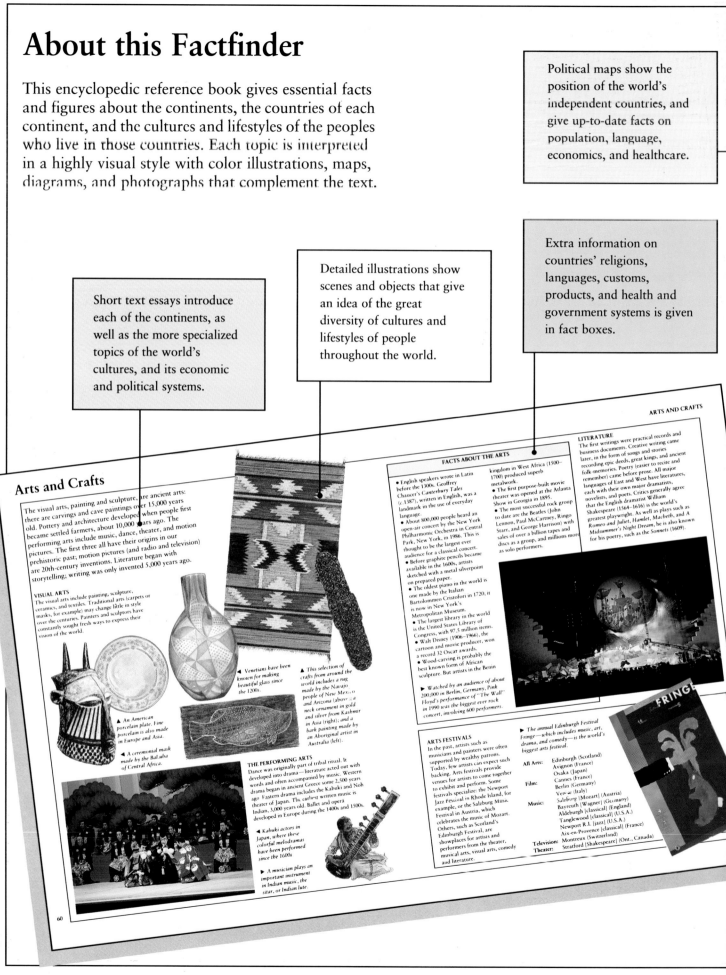

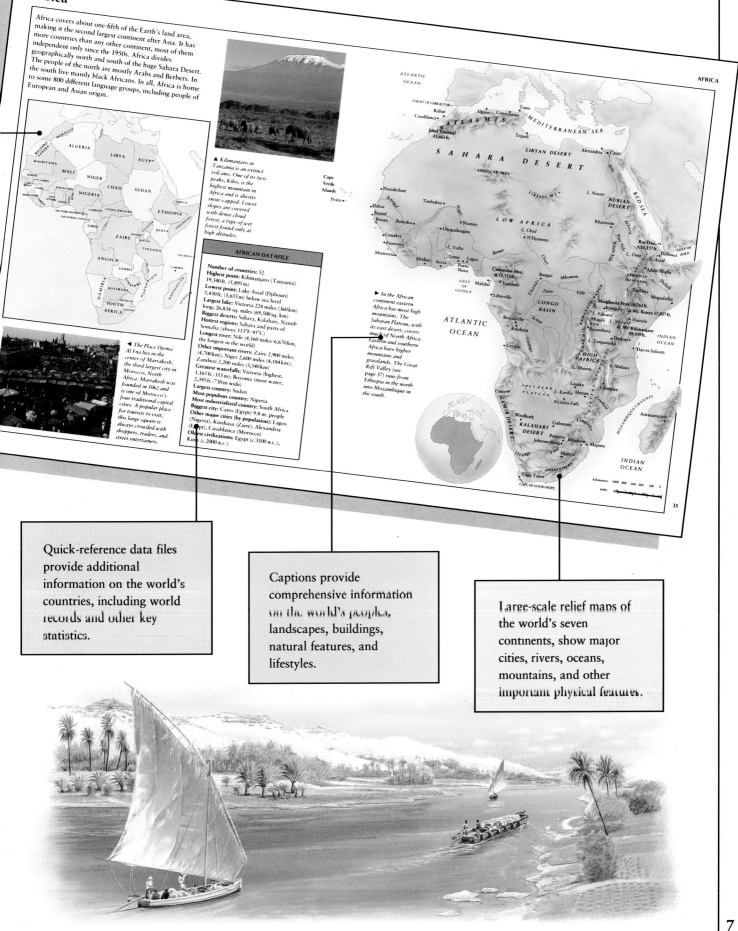

# Africa

Africa covers about one-fifth of the Earth's land area, making it the second largest continent after Asia. It has more countries than any other continent, most of them independent only since the 1950s. Africa divides geographically north and south of the huge Sahara Desert. The people of the north are mostly Arabs and Berbers. In the south live mainly black Africans. In all, Africa is home to some 800 different language groups, including people of European and Asian origin.

▲ Kilimanjaro in Tanzania is an extinct volcano. One of its two peaks, Kibo, is the highest mountain in Africa and is always snow-capped. Lower slopes are covered with dense cloud forest, a type of wet forest found only at high altitudes.

◄ The Place Djema Al Fna lies in the center of Marrakesh, the third largest city in Morocco, North Africa. Marrakesh was founded in 1062 and is one of Morocco's four traditional capital cities. A popular place for tourists to visit, this large square is always crowded with shoppers, traders, and street entertainers.

## AFRICAN DATAFILE

**Number of countries:** 52
**Highest point:** Kilimanjaro (Tanzania) 19,340 ft. (5,895 m)
**Lowest point:** Lake Assal (Djibouti) 5,430 ft. (1,655 m) below sea level
**Largest lake:** Victoria 224 miles (360 km) long; 26,834 sq. miles (69,500 sq. km)
**Biggest deserts:** Sahara, Kalahari, Namib
**Hottest regions:** Sahara and parts of Somalia (above 113°F/45°C)
**Longest river:** Nile (4,160 miles/6,670 km, the longest in the world)
**Other important rivers:** Zaire 2,900 miles (4,700 km); Niger 2,600 miles (4,184 km); Zambezi 2,200 miles (3,540 km)
**Greatest waterfalls:** Victoria (highest, 1,165 ft./355 m); Boyoma (most water, 2,395 ft./730 m wide)
**Largest country:** Sudan
**Most populous country:** Nigeria
**Most industrialized country:** South Africa
**Other major cities (by population):** Lagos (Nigeria), Kinshasa (Zaire), Alexandria (Egypt), Casablanca (Morocco)
**Oldest civilizations:** Egypt (c.3100 B.C.), Kush (c.2000 B.C.)

▶ In the African continent eastern Africa has most high mountains. The Saharan Plateau, with its vast desert, covers much of North Africa. Eastern and southern Africa have higher mountains and grasslands. The Great Rift Valley (see page 37) runs from Ethiopia in the north into Mozambique in the south.

Quick-reference data files provide additional information on the world's countries, including world records and other key statistics.

Captions provide comprehensive information on the world's peoples, landscapes, buildings, natural features, and lifestyles.

Large-scale relief maps of the world's seven continents, show major cities, rivers, oceans, mountains, and other important physical features.

*Every country has special festivals. These celebrations in Nigeria mark the end of Ramadan.*

# COUNTRIES
## OF THE
# WORLD

Facts about countries and people change all the time. Over the centuries, wars, revolutions, and independence movements have shaped our world. Countries have changed their names, merged with neighbors, gained or lost territory. And as countries change, so the culture and lifestyles of the world's peoples have also changed. In order for us to understand the world we live in, we need detailed knowledge, including key facts and figures, about its regions, countries, geography, and lifestyles. All this information is at your fingertips in *Countries of the World*.

In the world today many inequalities exist — in food, healthcare, resources, and income — and the North-South divide between the richer and poorer nations now overshadows the old East–West confrontation of the Cold War. In this book, two comprehensive sections provide a survey of the world's different economic and political systems and pinpoint key areas of 20th-century conflict. *Countries of the World* offers a ready-reference about the countries and peoples of today's rapidly changing world.

*Brian Williams*

# THE WORLD

## Continents and Countries

The Earth has existed for about 4.6 billion years, but modern humans, *Homo sapiens sapiens*, have been around for only 10,000 years. Civilizations did not begin to develop until 11,000 years ago, yet in that brief time people have spread to almost every habitable region, founding cultures and nations. Of the seven continents (Africa, Antarctica, Asia, Europe, North America, South America, and Oceania) only Antarctica has not been permanently settled. Asia is easily the biggest continent. It contains the most populous nation (China) and most of the biggest country by area (Russia). There are now more than 170 generally recognized independent countries in the world. Some are small islands such as Malta, Nauru, or Singapore, others are giant countries such as Australia, Canada, China, and the United States; each has its own cultural identity.

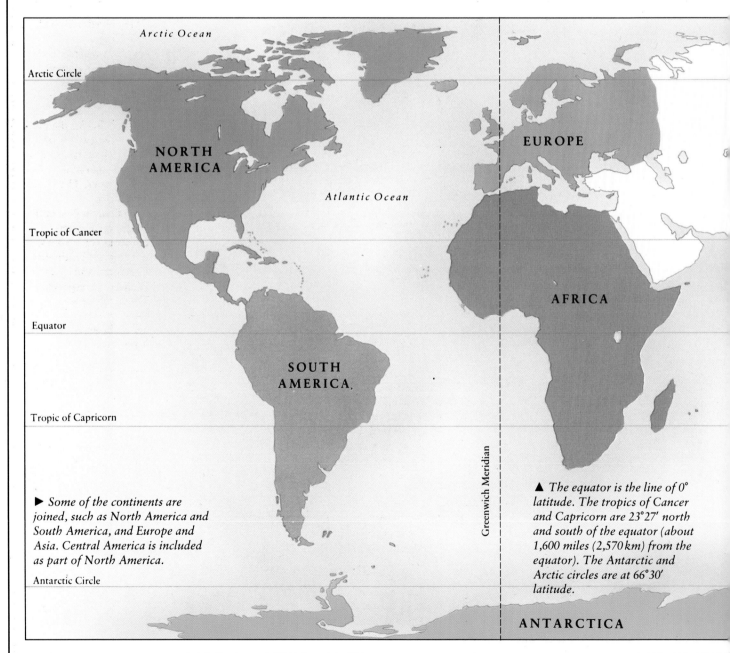

Arctic Ocean

Arctic Circle

NORTH AMERICA

EUROPE

Atlantic Ocean

Tropic of Cancer

AFRICA

Equator

SOUTH AMERICA

Tropic of Capricorn

Greenwich Meridian

▶ Some of the continents are joined, such as North America and South America, and Europe and Asia. Central America is included as part of North America.

▲ The equator is the line of 0° latitude. The tropics of Cancer and Capricorn are 23°27' north and south of the equator (about 1,600 miles (2,570 km) from the equator). The Antarctic and Arctic circles are at 66°30' latitude.

Antarctic Circle

ANTARCTICA

| CONTINENTS | AREA (Sq. Miles) | % OF WORLD'S LAND AREA | POPULATION (MILLIONS) | NUMBER OF COUNTRIES | LARGEST COUNTRY |
|---|---|---|---|---|---|
| NORTH AMERICA | 9,400,000 | 16.2 | 424 | 23 | Canada |
| SOUTH AMERICA | 6,900,000 | 11.9 | 298 | 12 | Brazil |
| EUROPE | 3,800,000 | 6.6 | 788[3] | 45[4] | Russia[1] |
| ASIA | 17,150,000 | 30.1 | 3173 | 44 | China |
| AFRICA | 11,700,000 | 20.2 | 657 | 52 | Sudan |
| OCEANIA | 3,300,000 | 5.7 | 26 | 11 | Australia |
| ANTARCTICA | 5,400,000 | 9.3 | none[2] | 0 | – |

[1] Part in Europe, part in Asia
[2] Population consists mainly of scientists
[3] Population includes Russia
[4] Number of countries includes 6 from the Commonwealth of Independent States, 3 Baltic states

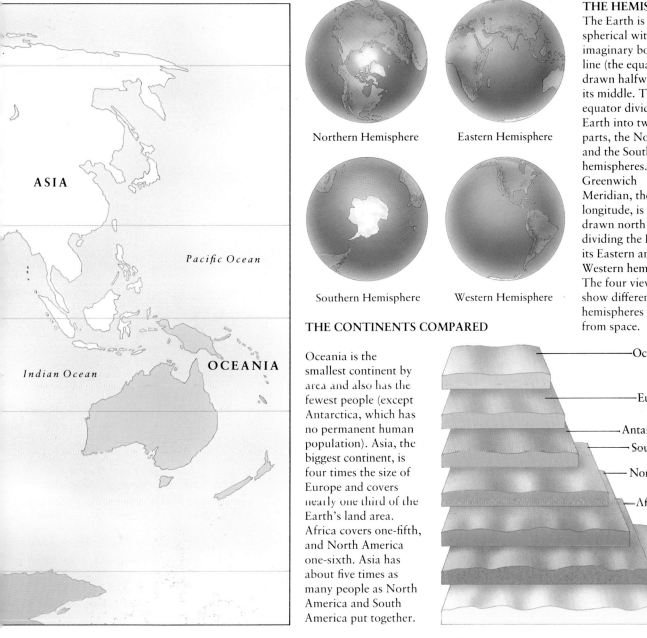

ASIA

Pacific Ocean

Indian Ocean

OCEANIA

Northern Hemisphere

Eastern Hemisphere

Southern Hemisphere

Western Hemisphere

## THE HEMISPHERES

The Earth is spherical with an imaginary boundary line (the equator) drawn halfway around its middle. The equator divides the Earth into two equal parts, the Northern and the Southern hemispheres. The Greenwich Meridian, the line of 0° longitude, is a line drawn north to south, dividing the Earth into its Eastern and Western hemispheres. The four views show different hemispheres as seen from space.

## THE CONTINENTS COMPARED

Oceania is the smallest continent by area and also has the fewest people (except Antarctica, which has no permanent human population). Asia, the biggest continent, is four times the size of Europe and covers nearly one third of the Earth's land area. Africa covers one-fifth, and North America one-sixth. Asia has about five times as many people as North America and South America put together.

Oceania 5.7%

Europe 6.6%

Antarctica 9.3%

South America 11.9%

North America 16.2%

Africa 20.2%

Asia 30.1%

11

# North America

North America is the world's third biggest continent, after Asia and Africa. It has a wide range of climates and landscapes, from the cold and snows of Alaska, northern Canada, and Greenland to the warmth of Central America and the Caribbean islands. The continent has two very large nations, the United States and Canada. The United States is the world's only superpower. The countries of Central America and the Caribbean are smaller than the U.S.A. and Canada, and many are comparatively poor.

▲ This lake is in the Canadian Rockies in Alberta, Canada. The Rocky Mountain chain is the major mountain system of North America. It stretches from New Mexico in the south to Alaska and the Yukon Territory of Canada.

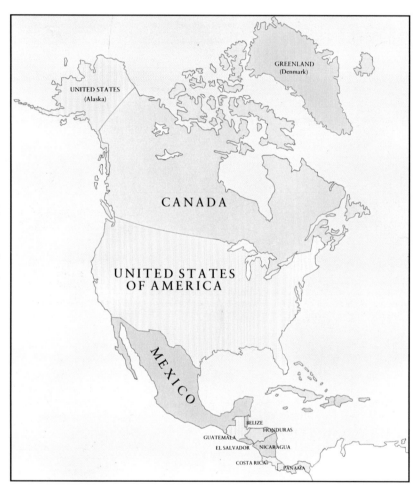

## NORTH AMERICAN DATAFILE

**Number of Countries:** 23
**Coastline:** 92,170 miles (148,330 km) long
**Highest mountain:** Mt. McKinley in Alaska, 20,320 ft. (6,194 m)
**Lowest point:** Death Valley, California, 282 ft. (86 m) below sea level
**Hottest place:** Amos, California, with a top temperature of 130°F (54.4°C) in 1885
**Coldest place:** Floeberg Bay, Canada, with a temperature of −72.4°F (−58°C) in 1852
**Longest rivers:** Mississippi, 2,348 miles (3,779 km), Missouri, 2,315 miles (3,726 km), Rio Grande, 1,885 miles (3,034 km), Arkansas, 1,459 miles (2,348 km)
**Largest lake:** Superior, between the U.S. and Canada; at 31,700 sq. miles (82,103 sq. km) the largest freshwater lake on Earth
**Largest city:** Mexico City (20 m people)
**Major cities (by population):** New York, Los Angeles, Chicago, Houston, Philadelphia, Toronto, Detroit

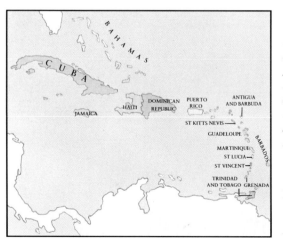

◄ The Caribbean islands form part of North America. There are three main island groups: the Bahamas, the Greater Antilles (Cuba, Jamaica, Haiti, Dominican Republic, and Puerto Rico), and the Lesser Antilles.

► Chicago is the third largest city in the U.S.A., as well as the birthplace of the skyscraper.

ARCTIC OCEAN

BERING SEA

Queen Elizabeth
Islands

GREENLAND

YUKON RIVER BASIN

Devon
Island

BAFFIN
BAY

Mt. McKinley
△ 20,320 ft.
ALASKA RANGE

Victoria
Island

Baffin Island

DAVIS STRAIT

GULF
OF
ALASKA

△ Mt. Logan
19,524 ft.

Yukon

Mackenzie

Great Bear
Lake

ATLANTIC OCEAN

Cape Farewell

Alexander
Archipelago

Great
Slave Lake

LABRADOR SEA

Queen
Charlotte
Islands

L. Athabasca

Reindeer
Lake

Edmonton

Calgary

Saskatchewan

HUDSON
BAY

Labrador

Vancouver

Seattle

Fraser

L Manitoba

L. Winnipeg

Nelson

GULF OF
ST. LAWRENCE

Cape
Breton
Island

Missouri

COAST RANGE

CASCADE RANGE

Snake

L. Superior

Quebec

Montreal

St. Lawrence

Great Salt
Lake

GREAT
BASIN

Sacramento

GREAT PLAINS

L. Huron

L. Michigan

Ottawa

Toronto

L. Ontario

Niagara Falls

Boston

San Francisco

Denver

Platte

Des Moines

Chicago

Detroit

L. Erie

New York

Philadelphia

SIERRA NEVADA

Death Valley

Colorado

Arkansas

Lincoln

Springfield

Ohio

Washington
D.C.

MOJAVE
DESERT

△ Mt. Elbert
14,432 ft.

Tennessee

APPALACHIAN MTS

CHESAPEAKE
BAY

Los Angeles

Phoenix

Nashville

PACIFIC OCEAN

EDWARDS
PLATEAU

Little Rock

Mississippi

△ Mt.
Mitchell
6,683 ft.

GULF OF
CALIFORNIA

SIERRA MADRE OCCIDENTAL

CHIHUAHUA DESERT

Dallas

Rio Grande

Houston

New Orleans

Miami

Nassau

Cape San Lucas

GULF OF
MEXICO

Havana

San Juan

▶ North America is
divided by the Rocky
Mountains, which
extend north to south.
The north of the
continent has many
lakes and rivers. The
Great Lakes include
Superior, the biggest
lake in North America.
The most important
river system is the
Mississippi-Missouri.

Paricutin
9,213 ft. △

Mexico City

△
Orizaba
18,700 ft.

Belmopan

Port-au-Prince

Santo Domingo

Kingston

CARIBBEAN SEA

Guatemala City

Tegucigalpa

San Salvador

Managua

San José

Panama City

Panama Canal

0  200  400  600  800 1000   kilometers

0      200      400      600    miles

| COUNTRY | AREA (sq. miles) | POPULATION | CAPITAL | LANGUAGE |
|---|---|---|---|---|
| Antigua and Barbuda | 171 | 64,000 | St. John's | English |
| Bahamas | 5,380 | 251,000 | Nassau | English |
| Barbados | 166 | 260,000 | Bridgetown | English |
| Belize | 8,867 | 180,400 | Belmopan | English, Spanish |
| Canada | 3,849,000 | 26,527,000 | Ottawa | English, French |
| Costa Rica | 19,575 | 3,032,000 | San José | Spanish |
| Cuba | 44,218 | 10,582,000 | Havana | Spanish |
| Dominica | 290 | 85,000 | Roseau | English |
| Dominican Republic | 18,816 | 7,253,000 | Santo Domingo | Spanish |
| El Salvador | 8,124 | 5,221,000 | San Salvador | Spanish, Nahuati |
| Grenada | 133 | 84,000 | St. George's | English |
| Guatemala | 42,042 | 9,340,000 | Guatemala City | Spanish, Indian languages |
| Haiti | 10,579 | 6,409,000 | Port-au-Prince | French, Creole |
| Honduras | 43,277 | 5,261,000 | Tegucigalpa | Spanish |
| Jamaica | 4,232 | 2,513,000 | Kingston | English, Creole |
| Mexico | 761,604 | 88,335,000 | Mexico City | Spanish |
| Nicaragua | 50,193 | 3,606,000 | Managua | Spanish, English |
| Panama | 29,208 | 2,423,000 | Panama City | Spanish |
| St. Kitts-Nevis | 101 | 44,000 | Basseterre | English |
| St. Lucia | 238 | 151,000 | Castries | English |
| St. Vincent and Grenadines | 150 | 115,000 | Kingstown | English |
| Trinidad and Tobago | 1,980 | 1,233,000 | Port of Spain | English |
| United States | 3,618,770 | 251,394,000 | Washington, D.C. | English |

### THE UNITED STATES OF AMERICA

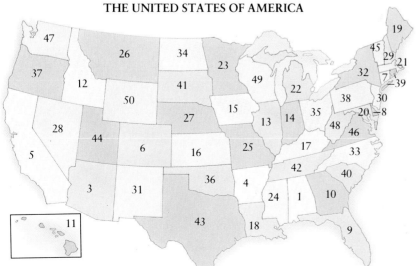

### U.S. STATES AND THEIR CAPITALS

| | | |
|---|---|---|
| 1 **Alabama** Montgomery | 11 **Hawaii** Honolulu | 21 **Massachusetts** Boston |
| 2 **Alaska** Juneau | 12 **Idaho** Boise | 22 **Michigan** Lansing |
| 3 **Arizona** Phoenix | 13 **Illinois** Springfield | 23 **Minnesota** St. Paul |
| 4 **Arkansas** Little Rock | 14 **Indiana** Indianapolis | 24 **Mississippi** Jackson |
| 5 **California** Sacramento | 15 **Iowa** Des Moines | 25 **Missouri** Jefferson City |
| 6 **Colorado** Denver | 16 **Kansas** Topeka | 26 **Montana** Helena |
| 7 **Connecticut** Hartford | 17 **Kentucky** Frankfort | 27 **Nebraska** Lincoln |
| 8 **Delaware** Dover | 18 **Louisiana** Baton Rouge | 28 **Nevada** Carson City |
| 9 **Florida** Tallahassee | 19 **Maine** Augusta | 29 **New Hampshire** Concord |
| 10 **Georgia** Atlanta | 20 **Maryland** Annapolis | 30 **New Jersey** Trenton |

14

| MAJOR PRODUCTS | CURRENCY |
|---|---|
| Tourism | EC Dollar |
| Tourism, rum, banking | C Dollar |
| Rum, molasses, tourism | Dollar |
| Sugar, timber | Dollar |
| Minerals, timber, cereals, factory goods | Dollar |
| Coffee | Dollar |
| Sugar, molasses, bananas, fish | Peso |
| Bananas, fruit, tourism | EC Dollar |
| Sugar, minerals | Peso |
| Coffee, cotton | Colon |
| Cocoa, nutmeg, bananas | EC Dollar |
| Coffee, minerals | Quetzal |
| Coffee, sugar | Gourde |
| Bananas, coffee, timber | Lempira |
| Bauxite, bananas, sugar, tourism | Dollar |
| Oil, minerals, textiles, steel | Peso |
| Coffee, cotton, meat | New Cordoba |
| Canal traffic, banking, bananas, rice, sugar | Balboa |
| Sugar, tourism | EC Dollar |
| Bananas, cocoa, textiles | EC Dollar |
| Bananas, arrowroot, tourism | EC Dollar |
| Oil, sugar, cocoa, coffee | Dollar |
| Foods, minerals, industrial goods | Dollar |

## THE ORIGINAL 13 U.S. COLONIES

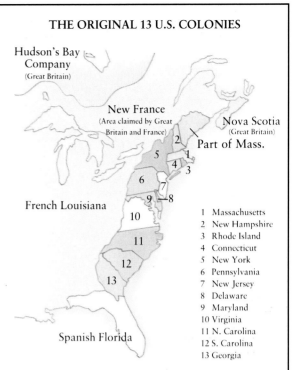

1 Massachusetts
2 New Hampshire
3 Rhode Island
4 Connecticut
5 New York
6 Pennsylvania
7 New Jersey
8 Delaware
9 Maryland
10 Virginia
11 N. Carolina
12 S. Carolina
13 Georgia

The United States grew from 13 colonies founded by British settlers in the 1600s. The first colony was Virginia, which was first permanently settled in 1607, followed by Massachusetts (1620), New Hampshire (1623), and New York (1624). Last of the 13 was Georgia (1733). The British colonies were on the east coast. To the west and south were French and Spanish territories. The 13 colonies broke away from British rule in 1776 in the historic Declaration of Independence.

## CANADA: PROVINCES AND TERRITORIES

PROVINCES
1 **Alberta**
 Edmonton
2 **British Columbia**
 Victoria
3 **Manitoba**
 Winnipeg

4 **New Brunswick**
 Fredericton
5 **Newfoundland**
 St. John's
6 **Nova Scotia**
 Halifax
7 **Ontario**
 Toronto

8 **Prince Edward Island**
 Charlottetown
9 **Quebec**
 Quebec City
10 **Saskatchewan**
 Regina
TERRITORIES
11 **Northwest Territories**
 Yellowknife
12 **Yukon**
 Whitehorse

31 **New Mexico**
 Santa Fé
32 **New York**
 Albany
33 **North Carolina**
 Raleigh
34 **North Dakota**
 Bismarck
35 **Ohio**
 Columbus
36 **Oklahoma**
 Oklahoma City
37 **Oregon**
 Salem
38 **Pennsylvania**
 Harrisburg
39 **Rhode Island**
 Providence
40 **South Carolina**
 Columbia

41 **South Dakota**
 Pierre
42 **Tennessee**
 Nashville
43 **Texas**
 Austin
44 **Utah**
 Salt Lake City
45 **Vermont**
 Montpelier
46 **Virginia**
 Richmond
47 **Washington**
 Olympia
48 **West Virginia**
 Charleston
49 **Wisconsin**
 Madison
50 **Wyoming**
 Cheyenne

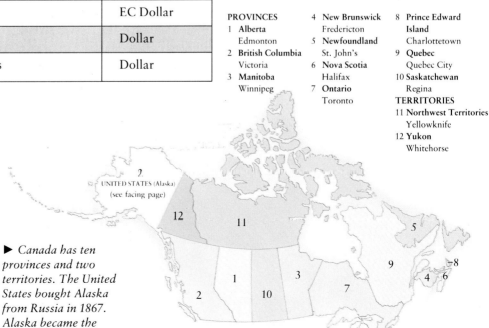

▶ *Canada has ten provinces and two territories. The United States bought Alaska from Russia in 1867. Alaska became the 49th U.S. state in 1959.*

# North America

North America is a continent of spectacle and superlatives, with some of the largest cities and most amazing natural wonders on Earth. Its peoples are as varied as its landscapes. The first Americans migrated from Asia thousands of years ago. Spreading across the great continent, they formed hunting and farming settlements and also built cities. Europeans first arrived in the 1500s, creating the United States of America in 1776. Canada became independent from the United Kingdom in 1867.

▲ The longest river in the United States, the Mississippi River carries more than 40 percent of U.S. inland freight.

▼ The city of St. Louis was once called the "Gateway to the West." The Gateway Arch is on the city's riverfront.

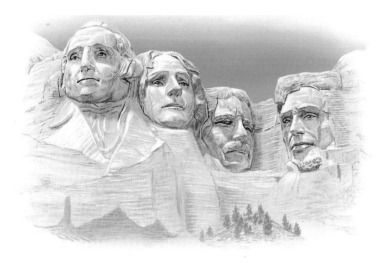

▲ The faces of four U.S. presidents are carved on a granite cliff at Mt. Rushmore, South Dakota.

◄ A weekly market on the Caribbean island of Grenada. Formerly a British colony, it became independent in 1974.

▲ The world's biggest radio telescope dish, measuring almost 1,000 ft. (305 m) across, is at Arecibo, Puerto Rico.

◄ The Grand Canyon in Arizona was cut by the Colorado River, and is the largest land gorge in the world.

► Old Faithful, in Yellowstone National Park, is a geyser that spouts hot water about 150 ft. (45 m) high every 70 minutes.

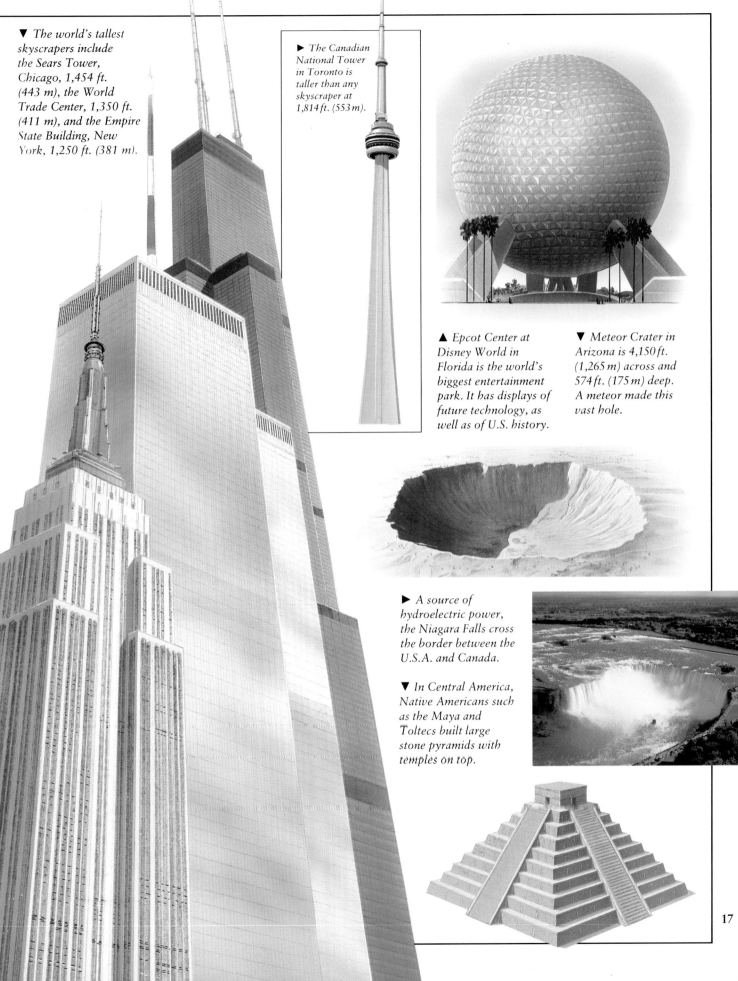

▼ *The world's tallest skyscrapers include the Sears Tower, Chicago, 1,454 ft. (443 m), the World Trade Center, 1,350 ft. (411 m), and the Empire State Building, New York, 1,250 ft. (381 m).*

▶ *The Canadian National Tower in Toronto is taller than any skyscraper at 1,814 ft. (553 m).*

▲ *Epcot Center at Disney World in Florida is the world's biggest entertainment park. It has displays of future technology, as well as of U.S. history.*

▼ *Meteor Crater in Arizona is 4,150 ft. (1,265 m) across and 574 ft. (175 m) deep. A meteor made this vast hole.*

▶ *A source of hydroelectric power, the Niagara Falls cross the border between the U.S.A. and Canada.*

▼ *In Central America, Native Americans such as the Maya and Toltecs built large stone pyramids with temples on top.*

# South America

The fourth largest continent, South America is the largest part of Latin America (where most people speak Spanish or Portuguese). Much of the continent is thinly populated, including the Amazon rain forest region and the high Andes Mountains. The central plains include grasslands, known as *llanos* in the north and *pampas* in the south. About 75 percent of South Americans are city dwellers. South America is rich in natural resources, but many people in both the cities and the country live in poverty.

▲ *The beautiful opera house in Manaus, Brazil, was built with money from the region's wild rubber boom of 1890–1912.*

▼ *In Argentina's capital of Buenos Aires, the artistic quarter of La Boca is celebrated for its painted houses.*

**THE AMAZON RAIN FOREST**
The Amazon rain forest is the world's greatest tropical forest and the home of thousands of species of birds, mammals, reptiles, and insects. There are also more than 40,000 varieties of plants. However, much of the rain forest has now been cleared by farmers and new settlers.

◄ *In South American countries such as Brazil, cattle raising is big business. Gauchos are the cowboys of the pampas, or plains. They are usually of mixed European and Indian blood.*

CARIBBEAN SEA

ATLANTIC OCEAN

Nevado del Ruiz 17,716 ft.

GULF OF PANAMA

PACIFIC OCEAN

Caracas

Orinoco

LLANOS

Angel Falls

Georgetown

Paramaribo

Cayenne

GUYANA HIGHLANDS

Magdalena

Bogotá

Maracá Island

Marajó Island

L. Maracaibo

Quito

Negro

Branco

Amazon

Cape Sao Roque

Chimborazo 20,561 ft.

Japurá

AMAZON RAINFOREST REGION

Tocantins

Paulo Afonso Falls

Meranon

Ucayli

Yavari

Purus

Madeira

Tapajós

Araguaia

Sao Francisco

Huascarán 22,188 ft.

Lima

MATO GROSSO

BRAZILIAN HIGHLANDS

A N D E S

Ucayali

SERRA DOS PARECIS

PLATEAU

Brasília

► *South America's two main geographical features are the Andes Mountains stretching down the western side of the continent, and the Amazon Basin with its great river systems. The windswept far south has few inhabitants.*

Coropuna 21,079 ft.

L. Titicaca

La Paz

El Misti 19,101 ft.

Sucre

GRAN CHACO

Rio de Janeiro

PACIFIC OCEAN

Lake Poopó

ATACAMA DESERT

Pilcomayo

Sao Paulo

Iguaçu Falls

Cape Frio

Ojos del Salado 22,572 ft.

Asunción

Iguaçu

A N D E S

Salado

Paraná

Uruguay

Mirim Lake

Cerro Aconcagua 22,830 ft.

Santiago

Buenos Aires

Montevideo

Tupungato 22,310 ft.

PAMPAS

RIO DE LA PLATA

Cape San Antonio

Negro

PATAGONIA

Los Chonos Archipelago

Cape Tres Puntas

kilometers 0 200 400 600 800 1000

miles 0 200 400 600

Falkland Islands

Reina Adelaida Archipelago

Tierra del Fuego

Strait of Magellan

South Georgia

Cape Horn

---

## SOUTH AMERICAN DATAFILE

**Number of countries:** 12
**Greatest mountains:** Andes, over 4,470 miles (7,200 km) long, longest range on Earth
**Highest point:** Cerro Aconcagua in Andes, 22,830 ft. (6,960 m)
**Driest spot:** Atacama Desert
**Longest river:** Amazon, 4,000 miles (6,448 km). Other important rivers: Magdalena, Orinoco
**Highest waterfall:** Angel Falls, 3,200 ft. (978 m)
**Biggest lake:** Maracaibo, in Venezuela, covering 6,293 sq. miles (16,300 sq. km); Titicaca at 12,500 ft. (3,812 m) is the highest lake in the world
**Biggest and most populous country:** Brazil
**Major cities (by population):** São Paulo, Rio de Janeiro, Buenos Aires, Lima, Bogotá

| COUNTRY | AREA (sq. miles) | POPULATION | CAPITAL | LANGUAGE |
|---|---|---|---|---|
| Argentina | 1,065,189 | 32,880,000 | Buenos Aires | Spanish |
| Bolivia | 424,165 | 7,400,000 | La Paz | Spanish, Aymara, Quechua |
| Brazil | 3,286,470 | 150,368,000 | Brasília | Portuguese |
| Chile | 292,257 | 13,173,000 | Santiago | Spanish |
| Colombia | 439,735 | 32,978,000 | Bogotá | Spanish |
| Ecuador | 109,483 | 10,782,000 | Quito | Spanish |
| Guyana | 83,000 | 756,000 | Georgetown | English, Hindi, Urdu |
| Paraguay | 157,047 | 4,277,000 | Asunción | Spanish |
| Peru | 496,222 | 22,332,000 | Lima | Spanish, Aymara, Quechua |
| Surinam | 63,037 | 411,000 | Paramaribo | Dutch |
| Uruguay | 68,037 | 3,033,000 | Montevideo | Spanish |
| Venezuela | 352,143 | 19,735,000 | Caracas | Spanish |

▲ The Andes Mountains rise along the western side of South America. They are the world's longest mountain chain, with many peaks over 20,000 ft. (6,000 m).

◄ A statue called Christ the Redeemer overlooks the bay at Rio de Janeiro, South America's finest natural harbor. Another of Rio's landmarks is Sugar Loaf Mountain.

▲ Reed boats on Lake Titicaca, the highest navigable lake in the world. The Atacama Desert (below) is the driest area in South America, stretching from southern Peru into northern Chile.

| MAJOR PRODUCTS AND INDUSTRIES | CURRENCY |
|---|---|
| Cereals, wool, vegetable oils, meat | Austral |
| Natural gas, metals (zinc, tin, gold) | Peso |
| Coffee, sugar, cattle, textiles | Cruzeiro |
| Copper, fruit, fish meal, paper | Peso |
| Coffee, bananas, minerals | Peso |
| Petroleum, shrimps, bananas | Sucre |
| Bauxite, sugar, rice | Dollar |
| Cotton, soybeans, meat, coffee, timber | Guarani |
| Coffee, sugar, minerals | Inti |
| Aluminum, shrimps, rice | Surinam Guilder |
| Textiles, meat, hides | New Peso |
| Petroleum, natural gas | Bolívar |

◄ *The cathedral in Brasília. The city was built to be capital of Brazil, replacing Rio de Janeiro.*

▲ *The Angel Falls: water plummets down a cliff on Mount Auyantepui in south-east Venezuela.*

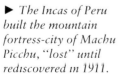

► *The Incas of Peru built the mountain fortress-city of Machu Picchu, "lost" until rediscovered in 1911.*

► *The Ambato market in Quito, the second largest city of Ecuador. Quito is famous for its weekly outdoor markets; held in different parts of the city, they attract large crowds. Most of the city's markets specialize in particular types of goods.*

# Europe

Europe is the second smallest of the continents, yet only Asia has more people. Europe is therefore the most crowded continent. It is the birthplace of Western civilization, and through trade, cultural contact, and colonization has had an immense influence on the world. Its map has been redrawn many times in history. Changes in the 1990s include the growth of the European Community; the unification of Germany; and the break up of the Soviet Union, Czechoslovakia, and Yugoslavia.

## EUROPEAN DATAFILE

**Number of countries:** 45
**Population:** 788,000,000
**Biggest cities (by pop.):** Moscow (Russia) 8,967,000; Paris (France) 8,707,000; London (U.K.) 6,735,000
**Highest point:** Mt. Elbrus in Caucasus range in Russia, 18,480 ft. (5,633 m)
**Lowest point:** shore of Caspian Sea, 92 ft. (28 m) below sea level
**Longest river:** Volga, Russia, 2,194 miles (3,531 km). The Danube flows through Germany, Austria, Czechoslovakia, Hungary, Serbia, Bulgaria, Romania
**Biggest lake:** Caspian Sea 169,380 sq. miles (438,695 sq. km)
**Largest country:** Russia
**Biggest island:** Great Britain (England, Wales, and Scotland), 84,186 sq. miles (218,041 sq. km)

▶ *Europe is the western part of the Eurasia land mass. It extends eastward from the Atlantic Ocean to the Urals and contains about 20 percent of the world's population.*

BARENTS SEA

Reykjavik

Murmansk

NORWEGIAN SEA

Faeroe Islands

Shetland Islands

Orkney Islands

GULF OF BOTHNIA

Glittertind 8,104 ft.

Ullma

Dalälven

Helsinki
Oslo
St. Petersburg
Stockholm
Tallin

Ben Nevis 4,406 ft.

Belfast
Edinburgh

NORTH SEA

BALTIC SEA

Copenhagen
Riga
Neman
Vilnius

Dublin

IRISH SEA

Severn
Cardiff
London
Thames

Hamburg
Amsterdam
The Hague
Elbe
Berlin
Oder

Vistula
Bug
Uzh

Minsk

ENGLISH CHANNEL

Brussels

Warsaw

Seine
Paris

Rhine

Frankfurt
Luxembourg

Prague

BAY OF BISCAY

Loire
Allier
Yonne

Munich
Vienna

CARPATHIANS

ATLANTIC OCEAN

Bordeaux

MASSIF CENTRAL

Bern
Vaduz
ALPS

Budapest

Danube

Rhone

Matterhorn 14,691 ft.
Mt. Blanc 15,771 ft.
Po

Venice
Ljubljana
Zagreb

Belgrade

Bucharest

Douro

PYRENEES
Ebro

Marseille
Monaco

DINARIC ALPS

Sarajevo

BALKAN MTS.

Tejo
Madrid
Andorra

ADRIATIC SEA

Tavere

Sofia

Lisbon

Barcelona

Corsica

Tavere

Rome

APENNINES

Tirana

Mt Olympus 9,570 ft.

Balearic Islands

Sardinia

TYRRHENIAN SEA

Naples

AEGEAN

Gibraltar

Guadalquivir

MEDITERRANEAN SEA

Sicily

Malta

Athens

Crete

| 0 | 200 | 400 | 600 | 800 | Kilometers |
| 0 | 100 | 200 | 300 | 400 | 500 | Miles |

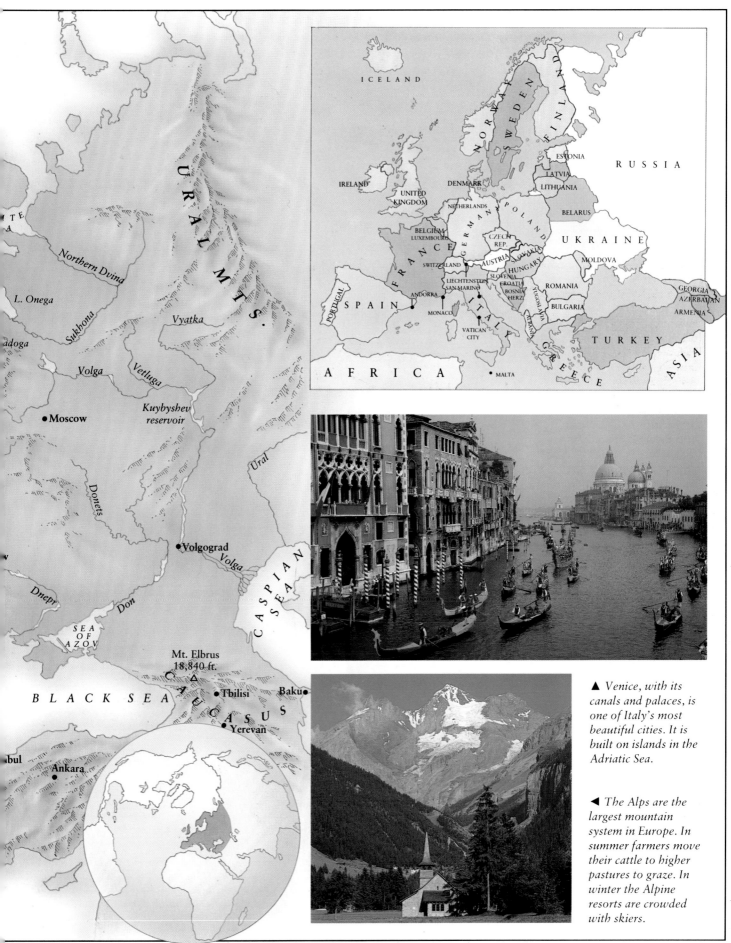

URAL MTS.

Northern Dvina

L. Onega

Sukhona

Vyatka

Vetluga

Kuybyshev reservoir

● Moscow

Volga

Ural

Donets

● Volgograd

Volga

Dnepr

Don

CASPIAN SEA

SEA OF AZOV

Mt. Elbrus 18,840 ft.

B L A C K   S E A

CAUCASUS

● Tbilisi

● Baku

● Yerevan

●bul

● Ankara

ICELAND

NORWAY

SWEDEN

FINLAND

IRELAND

UNITED KINGDOM

DENMARK

ESTONIA

LATVIA

LITHUANIA

RUSSIA

NETHERLANDS

BELGIUM

LUXEMBOURG

FRANCE

GERMANY

POLAND

BELARUS

UKRAINE

CZECH REP.

AUSTRIA

SLOVAKIA

HUNGARY

MOLDOVA

SWITZERLAND

LIECHTENSTEIN

SAN MARINO

SLOVENIA

CROATIA

ROMANIA

GEORGIA

AZERBAIJAN

PORTUGAL

SPAIN

ANDORRA

MONACO

ITALY

BOSNIA HERZ.

YUGOSLAVIA

BULGARIA

ARMENIA

VATICAN CITY

ALBANIA

GREECE

TURKEY

ASIA

AFRICA

● MALTA

▲ *Venice, with its canals and palaces, is one of Italy's most beautiful cities. It is built on islands in the Adriatic Sea.*

◄ *The Alps are the largest mountain system in Europe. In summer farmers move their cattle to higher pastures to graze. In winter the Alpine resorts are crowded with skiers.*

23

| COUNTRY | AREA (sq. miles) | POPULATION | CAPITAL | LANGUAGE |
|---|---|---|---|---|
| Albania | 11,100 | 3,278,000 | Tirana | Albanian |
| Andorra | 185 | 50,900 | Andorra la Vella | Catalan, French, Spanish |
| Armenia | 11,506 | 3,376,000 | Yerevan | Armenian, Russian |
| Austria | 32,374 | 7,623,000 | Vienna | German |
| Azerbaijan | 33,436 | 7,137,000 | Baku | Azerbaijani, Russian |
| Belarus | 80,154 | 10,260,000 | Minsk | Byelrussian, Russian |
| Belgium | 11,780 | 9,958,000 | Brussels | Flemish, French |
| Bosnia-Herzegovina | 19,741 | 4,479,000 | Sarajevo | Serbo-Croatian |
| Bulgaria | 42,823 | 8,997,000 | Sofia | Bulgarian, Turkish |
| Croatia | 21,829 | 4,683,000 | Zagreb | Croato-Serbian |
| Czech Republic | 30,450 | 10,299,000 | Prague | Czech |
| Denmark | 16,633 | 5,139,000 | Copenhagen | Danish |
| Estonia | 17,413 | 1,573,000 | Tallin | Estonian |
| Finland | 130,120 | 4,978,000 | Helsinki | Finnish |
| France | 220,668 | 56,647,000 | Paris | French |
| Georgia | 43,307 | 16,538,000 | Tbilisi | Georgian, Russian |
| Germany | 137,838 | 78,000,000 | Berlin | German |
| Greece | 51,146 | 10,141,000 | Athens | Greek |
| Hungary | 35,910 | 10,563,000 | Budapest | Hungarian |
| Iceland | 39,768 | 256,000 | Reykjavik | Icelandic |
| Ireland | 27,136 | 3,509,000 | Dublin | Irish, English |
| Italy | 116,303 | 57,512,000 | Rome | Italian |
| Latvia | 24,595 | 2,681,000 | Riga | Latvian, Russian |
| Liechtenstein | 62 | 28,700 | Vaduz | German |
| Lithuania | 25,170 | 3,690,000 | Vilnius | Lithuanian |
| Luxembourg | 998 | 379,000 | Luxembourg | Letzeburgish, French |
| Malta | 122 | 353,000 | Valletta | Maltese, English |
| Moldova | 13,012 | 4,341,000 | Kishinev | Moldovian, Russian |
| Monaco | 0.6 | 29,300 | Monaco | French, Monegasque |
| Netherlands | 15,770 | 14,934,000 | Amsterdam | Dutch |
| Norway | 125,181 | 4,246,000 | Oslo | Norwegian (two forms) |
| Poland | 120,725 | 38,064,000 | Warsaw | Polish |
| Portugal | 35,553 | 10,388,000 | Lisbon | Portuguese |

| MAJOR PRODUCTS AND INDUSTRIES | CURRENCY |
|---|---|
| Minerals, food products | Lek |
| Tourism, consumer goods | Spanish Peseta |
| Chemicals, agriculture, machinery | Ruble |
| Machinery, consumer goods, tourism | Schilling |
| Oil, iron, steel, textiles | Ruble |
| Livestock, timber | Ruble |
| Metals, textiles, chemicals, ceramics | Franc |
| Agriculture, chemicals, machinery | Dinar |
| Foods, wine, tobacco | Lev |
| Agriculture, machinery, clothing, textiles | Dinar |
| Machinery, vehicles, consumer goods | Koruna |
| Dairy foods, beer, chemicals | Krone |
| Petroleum, fertilizer, timber, machinery | Kroon |
| Wood products, engineering, fish | Markka |
| Foods, wine, engineering, consumer goods | Franc |
| Mining, agriculture | Ruble |
| Engineering, chemicals, textiles, vehicles | Deutsch Mark |
| Foods, clothing, petroleum products | Drachma |
| Machinery, foods, consumer goods | Forint |
| Fish | Krona |
| Manufactured goods, foods | Irish Pound |
| Foods, wine, textiles, engineering, vehicles | Lira |
| Machinery, electrical equipment, processed foods | Lat |
| Tourism, banking, precision engineering | Swiss Franc |
| Chemicals, metal goods, electrical equipment | Litas |
| Iron and steel | Luxembourg Fr. |
| Ship repair, tourism | Maltese Lira |
| Agriculture, foods, chemicals | Ruble |
| Property, banking, tourism | Franc |
| Foods, flowers, manufacturing, natural gas | Guilder |
| Natural gas, petroleum, timber, fish | Krone |
| Machinery, chemicals, foods, textiles | Zloty |
| Foods, fish, cork, textiles, manufacturing | Escudo |

## THE EUROPEAN COMMUNITY

Twelve countries belong to the European Community (EC), and other European countries are seeking membership. Appointed by countries of the EC, the Commission meets in Brussels, Belgium. Here its members plan policy for the Community, now developing from a free trade area into a more close-knit political organization.

◄ *The EC Commission is the body that initiates Community proposals. Its headquarters are in Brussels, Belgium.*

## CHANGES IN EASTERN EUROPE

The old Soviet Union of 15 republics broke up in 1990–1991. First to leave were the Baltic states of Estonia, Latvia, and Lithuania. The Slav states are Russia, Ukraine, and Belarus (Byelorussia). The Transcaucasian republics are Armenia, Georgia, and Azerbaijan. Moldova is by language and history part of Romania. The central Asian republics were in the pre-1917 Russian empire.

▲ *The Soviet Union broke into 15 separate republics. By far the biggest is Russia, most of which is in Asia.*

▼ *The Hermitage Museum, once the Winter Palace, is in St. Petersburg (formerly Leningrad).*

| COUNTRY | AREA (sq. miles) | POPULATION | CAPITAL | LANGUAGE |
|---|---|---|---|---|
| Romania | 91,700 | 23,265,000 | Bucharest | Romanian, Hungarian |
| Russia | 6,592,818 | 147,386,000 | Moscow | Russian |
| San Marino | 24 | 23,000 | San Marino | Italian |
| Slovak Republic | 18,932 | 5,269,000 | Bratislava | Slovak |
| Slovenia | 7,819 | 1,943,000 | Ljubljana | Slovenian |
| Spain | 194,896 | 38,959,000 | Madrid | Spanish, Catalan |
| Sweden | 173,731 | 8,529,000 | Stockholm | Swedish |
| Switzerland | 15,941 | 6,756,000 | Bern | German, French, Italian, Romansch |
| Ukraine | 233,089 | 51,800,000 | Kiev | Ukrainian, Russian |
| United Kingdom | 94,226 | 57,384,000 | London | English |
| Vatican City | 109 acres | 750 | Vatican City | Italian, Latin |
| *Yugoslavia (former) | 98,766 | 8,590,000 | Belgrade | Serbo-Croatian |

*By 1992 the federal republic of Yugoslavia had ceased to exist. At the time of printing the civil war in Bosnia continues. Macedonia has now been recognised as an independent country.

► *Amsterdam is the capital city of the Netherlands; it is built on islands, separated by its famous canals.*

◄ *The Lloyds Building was designed by Richard Rogers and finished in 1986. It lies in the City of London, the financial heart of the U.K. and an important world trading center.*

▲ *The Eiffel Tower in Paris was built in 1889 to mark one hundred years since the French Revolution.*

◄ *Running through the Alps, the St. Gotthard tunnel in Switzerland is the world's longest road tunnel.*

| MAJOR PRODUCTS AND INDUSTRIES | CURRENCY |
|---|---|
| Minerals, manufacturing, timber | Lev |
| Manufacturing, tourism | Ruble |
| Corn, pigs, steel, factory goods | Italian Lira |
| Agriculture, food products, wood products | Koruna |
| (Not available) | Dinar |
| Foods, wine, manufacturing, banking | Peseta |
| Uranium, iron, timber, pulp, engineering | Krona |
| Manufacturing, engineering, banking | Franc |
| Heavy industry, agriculture | Grivna |
| Manufacturing, petroleum, banking, tourism | Pound |
| None | Lira |
| Agriculture, clothing, textiles | Dinar |

▲ The world's tallest statue, "Motherland," 270 ft. (82 m), is in Volgograd, Russia.

▲ The city of Krakow, once capital of Poland, has many historic buildings in its center.

▼ Stonehenge, a 4,000-year-old English stone monument, is believed to have been a temple.

◄ These vineyards are in Tuscany, a region of Italy noted for its beauty. Italy is the EC's leading wine producer, followed by France and Spain.

▲ The spire of Ulm Cathedral in southern Germany is the highest spire in the world at almost 528 ft. (161 m).

▼ On the Acropolis in Athens stands the Parthenon, the most famous temple built by the ancient Greeks.

# Asia

About 60 percent of the Earth's population lives in Asia. The largest of all the continents, Asia has the world's highest mountains as well as great rivers, deserts, plains, polar wastes, forests, and tropical jungles. The world's great religions began in Asia, as did the first great civilizations. Since World War II (1939–1945), Asia has seen an economic boom in the Middle East and Japan; war in Korea, Vietnam, and the Middle East; and poverty made worse by natural disasters such as flooding in Bangladesh.

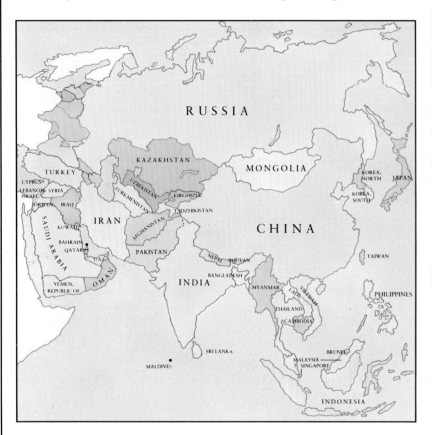

## ASIAN DATAFILE

**Number of countries:** 44
**Highest point:** Mt. Everest, 29,028 ft. (8,848 m). Next highest points: K2, 28,250 ft. (8,611 m), Mt. Kanchenjunga, 28,208 ft. (8,597 m)
**Longest river:** Chang Jiang (Yangtze), 3,964 miles (6,379 km)
**Other major rivers:** Ob-Irtysh 3,362 miles (5,410 km), Huang He 2,903 miles (4,672 km), Lena 2,734 miles (4,400 km), Mekong 2,600 miles (4,180 km)
**Lowest point:** Dead Sea shore, 1,309 ft. (399 m) below sea level

**Largest deserts:** Gobi, Kara Kum, Rub al Khali
**Largest lake:** Caspian Sea, 143,244 sq. miles (371,000 sq. km)
**Biggest country (excluding Russia, which is partly in Europe):** China
**Most populous country:** China
**Biggest city:** Tokyo-Yokohama (Japan). Other major cities (by population): Seoul (South Korea), Osaka-Kobe-Kyoto (Japan), Bombay and Calcutta (India), Manila (Philippines); all over 9.5 million people

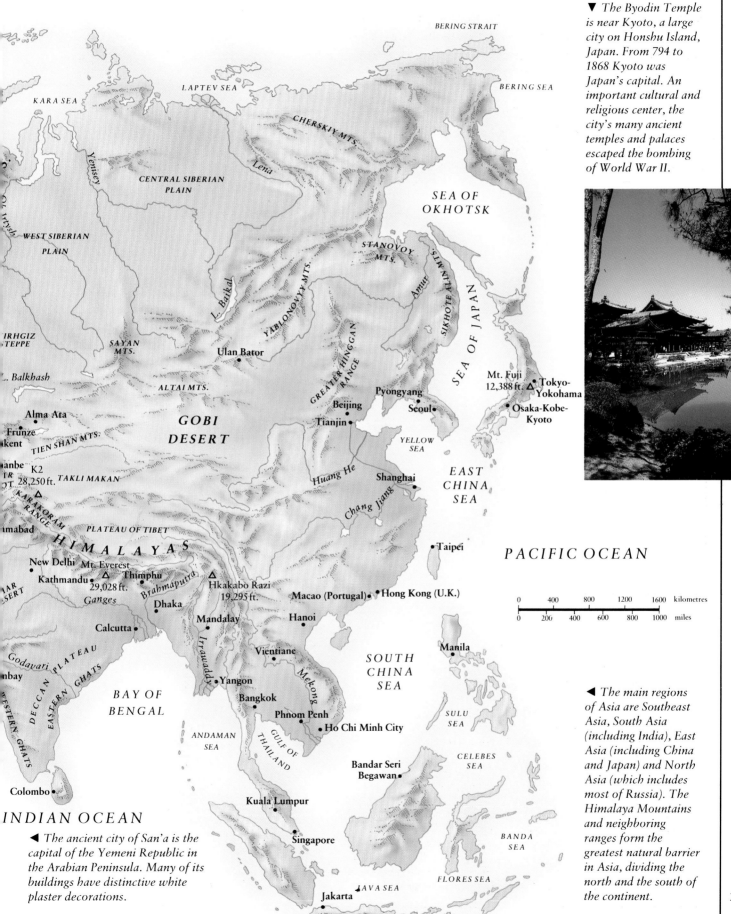

KARA SEA

LAPTEV SEA

BERING STRAIT

BERING SEA

OZ Irtysh

Yenisey

CENTRAL SIBERIAN PLAIN

Lena

CHERSKIY MTS.

SEA OF OKHOTSK

WEST SIBERIAN PLAIN

L. Baikal

YABLONOVYY MTS.

SAYAN MTS.

STANOVOY MTS.

Amur

SIKHOTE ALIN MTS.

IRHGIZ TEPPE

GREATER HINGAN RANGE

SEA OF JAPAN

L. Balkhash

ALTAI MTS.

Ulan Bator

Mt. Fuji 12,388 ft. △ Tokyo-Yokohama

Alma Ata

GOBI DESERT

Pyongyang

Beijing

Seoul

Osaka-Kobe-Kyoto

Frunze

kent

TIEN SHAN MTS.

Tianjin

anbe

K2

IR 28,250 ft.

TAKLI MAKAN

YELLOW SEA

Huang He

Shanghai

EAST CHINA SEA

KARAKORAM RANGE

amabad

PLATEAU OF TIBET

Chang Jiang

HIMALAYAS

New Delhi Mt. Everest

Kathmandu △ Thimphu

29,028 ft.

Brahmaputra

△ Hkakabo Razi 19,295 ft.

Taipei

PACIFIC OCEAN

Ganges

Dhaka

Macao (Portugal) ● Hong Kong (U.K.)

WAR

ESERT

Calcutta

Mandalay

Hanoi

| 0 | 400 | 800 | 1200 | 1600 | kilometres |
| 0 | 200 | 400 | 600 | 800 | 1000 | miles |

Godavari

DECCAN PLATEAU

EASTERN GHATS

Irrawaddy

Vientiane

Mekong

Manila

mbay

Yangon

SOUTH CHINA SEA

WESTERN GHATS

BAY OF BENGAL

Bangkok

Phnom Penh

● Ho Chi Minh City

SULU SEA

ANDAMAN SEA

GULF OF THAILAND

CELEBES SEA

Colombo

Bandar Seri Begawan

BANDA SEA

INDIAN OCEAN

Kuala Lumpur

Singapore

JAVA SEA

FLORES SEA

Jakarta

| COUNTRY | AREA (sq. miles) | POPULATION | CAPITAL | LANGUAGE |
|---|---|---|---|---|
| Afghanistan | 251,773 | 15,592,000 | Kabul | Pushto, Dari |
| Bahrain | 258 | 503,000 | Manama | Arabic |
| Bangladesh | 55,598 | 113,005,000 | Dhaka | Bengali |
| Bhutan | 18,147 | 1,442,000 | Thimphu | Dzongkha |
| Brunei | 2,226 | 258,000 | Bandar Seri Begawan | Malay |
| Cambodia | 69,898 | 8,592,000 | Phnom Penh | Khmer, French |
| China | 3,696,100 | 1,133,683,000 | Beijing | Mandarin Chinese |
| Cyprus[1] | 3,572 | 739,000 | Nicosia | Greek, Turkish |
| India | 1,266,595 | 853,373,000 | New Delhi | Hindi, English and others |
| Indonesia | 735,268 | 180,783,000 | Jakarta | Bahasa Indonesia |
| Iran | 636,293 | 56,923,000 | Tehran | Farsi, Azerbaijani |
| Iraq | 167,924 | 17,754,000 | Baghdad | Arabic, Kirdish |
| Israel[2] | 7,847 | 4,666,000 | Jerusalem | Hebrew, Arabic |
| Japan | 145,856 | 123,700,000 | Tokyo | Japanese |
| Jordan | 37,737 | 3,169,000 | Amman | Arabic |
| Kazakhstan | 1,049,150 | 16,793,000 | Alma Ata | Turkic |
| Kirghizia | 76,641 | 4,291,000 | Bishek | Turkic |
| Korea, North | 46,540 | 22,937,000 | Pyongyang | Korean |
| Korea, South | 38,025 | 42,791,000 | Seoul | Korean |
| Kuwait | 6,880 | 2,143,000 | Kuwait City | Arabic |
| Laos | 91,428 | 4,024,000 | Vientiane | Lao |
| Lebanon | 4,015 | 2,965,000 | Beirut | Arabic |
| Malaysia | 127,316 | 17,886,000 | Kuala Lumpur | Bahasa Malaysia |
| Maldives | 115 | 214,000 | Male | Divehi |
| Mongolia | 604,247 | 2,150,000 | Ulan Bator | Mongolian |
| Myanmar | 261,217 | 41,675,000 | Yangon | Burmese |
| Nepal | 56,136 | 18,910,000 | Kathmandu | Nepali |
| Oman | 82,030 | 1,468,000 | Muscat | Arabic |
| Pakistan | 310,403 | 122,666,000 | Islamabad | Urdu |
| Philippines | 115,830 | 61,483,000 | Manila | Filipino, English |
| Qatar | 4,247 | 444,000 | Doha | Arabic |
| Saudi Arabia | 839,996 | 14,131,000 | Riyadh | Arabic |
| Singapore | 224 | 2,702,000 | Singapore City | Chinese, English, Malay, Tamil |

| MAJOR PRODUCTS AND INDUSTRIES | CURRENCY |
|---|---|
| Cereals, dried fruit, wool, cotton | Afghani |
| Petroleum, natural gas | Dinar |
| Rice, jute, tea | Taka |
| Foods, timber | Ngultrum |
| Natural gas, petroleum | Brunei Dollar |
| Rice | Riel |
| Rice, minerals, fish, manufactured goods | Yuan |
| Foods, wine, tourism | Pound |
| Tea, cotton, sugar, jute, coal, manufactured goods | Rupee |
| Petroleum, natural gas | Rupiah |
| Petroleum, textiles, carpets | Rial |
| Petroleum, dates | Dinar |
| Fruit, vegetables, tourism | Sheqel |
| Vehicles, machinery, chemicals, textiles, electronics | Yen |
| Potash | Dinar |
| Cereals, cotton, petroleum | Rouble |
| Cotton | Rouble |
| Minerals, foods, textiles | Won |
| Vehicles, textiles, ships, steel, fish | Won |
| Petroleum, chemicals, fertilizer | Dinar |
| Farm products, timber, coffee, tin | Kip |
| Jewelry, clothes, pharmaceuticals | Lebanese Pound |
| Manufactured goods, palm oil, petroleum, rubber, tin | Malaysian Dollar |
| Fish, clothing | Rupee |
| Coal, metals, farm products | Tugrik |
| Teak, rice | Kyat Main |
| Foods, manufactured goods | Rupee |
| Petroleum | Rial |
| Cotton, textiles, foods, chemicals | Rupee |
| Electronics, clothing, farm products, wood | Peso |
| Petroleum, chemicals | Riyal |
| Petroleum | Riyal |
| Communications equipment, clothing, petroleum | Singapore Dollar |

## THE INDIAN SUBCONTINENT

Civilization in the Indian subcontinent began in the Indus Valley, about 5,500 years ago. In the 300–500s and the 1500s–1700s Hindu and Islamic (Mogul) rulers created powerful empires. Between the 1700s and 1947 most of this territory was part of British-controlled India. In 1947 India (mostly Hindu) and Pakistan (Islamic) went their separate ways as independent republics. Bangladesh, formerly East Pakistan, broke away to gain its independence in 1971.

▲ *Devout Indian Hindus come to bathe in the sacred river Ganges at Varanasi (Benares).*

▼ *The Taj Mahal in India was built (1630–1650) by the Mogul emperor Shah Jahan as a tomb for his wife.*

31

| COUNTRY | AREA (sq. miles) | POPULATION | CAPITAL | LANGUAGE |
|---|---|---|---|---|
| Sri Lanka | 25,332 | 17,103,000 | Colombo | Sinhalese, Tamil |
| Syria | 71,498 | 12,116,000 | Damascus | Arabic |
| Tadzhikistan | 55,251 | 5,358,000 | Dushanbe | Tadzhik |
| Taiwan | 13,885 | 20,262,000 | Taipei | Chinese |
| Thailand | 198,456 | 56,147,000 | Bangkok | Thai |
| Turkey | 301,381 | 56,941,000 | Ankara | Turkish |
| Turkmenistan | 188,455 | 3,622,000 | Ashkhabad | Turkic |
| Uzbekistan | 172,741 | 20,708,000 | Tashkent | Uzbek |
| United Arab Emirates | 32,000 | 1,881,000 | Abu Dhabi | Arabic |
| Vietnam | 127,330 | 66,111,000 | Hanoi | Vietnamese |
| Yemen | 205,356 | 11,546,000 | San'a | Arabic |

▼ *The Hindu temple of Angkor Wat, Cambodia, (built in 1113– 1150) is the world's largest religious structure.*

▼ *The port of Singapore is the key to the small city-state's economic prosperity.*

▲ *The Forbidden City was the central part of the Chinese emperor's palace in Beijing.*

| MAJOR PRODUCTS AND INDUSTRIES | CURRENCY |
|---|---|
| Tea, rubber, gemstones | Rupee |
| Petroleum, chemicals, textiles | Pound |
| Cotton | Rouble |
| Electronics, clothes, plastic goods | Taiwan Dollar |
| Textiles, rice, rubber, tapioca, teak | Baht |
| Textiles, foods, metals | Lira |
| Cotton | Rouble |
| Cotton | Rouble |
| Petroleum | Dirham |
| Coal, farm produce, livestock, fish | Dong |
| Coffee, hides, foods, cigarettes | Dinar, Riyal |

[1] Divided since 1974. Turkish Republic of Northern Cyprus not recognized by UN.
[2] Excludes territory occupied in 1967 war.
[3] 9,175 sq. miles (23,764 sq. km) in Europe.

▲ Oil has made some Middle Eastern states very rich, despite their lack of other resources. This refinery is in Saudi Arabia, the largest oil producer in the region.

▼ This train is on the Trans-Siberian Railroad, which runs from Moscow in Europe to Vladivostock in Asia. It is the world's longest railroad.

◄ A bullet-shaped Japanese high-speed electric train. Japan's highly efficient rail network includes the world's longest rail tunnel, the Seikan Tunnel (34 miles long); the first test run took place in 1988.

◄ The Great Wall of China, at 1,500 miles, is the longest structure ever built. First built as a defensive wall c.210 B.C.

► Jerusalem is a city sacred to Christians, Jews, and Muslims. Since 1967 the whole city has been occupied by Israel, whose capital it is.

# Africa

Africa covers about one-fifth of the Earth's land area, making it the second largest continent after Asia. It has more countries than any other continent, most of them independent only since the 1950s. Africa divides geographically north and south of the huge Sahara Desert. The people of the north are mostly Arabs and Berbers. In the south live mainly black Africans. In all, Africa is home to some 800 different language groups, including people of European and Asian origin.

▲ *Kilimanjaro in Tanzania is an extinct volcano. One of its two peaks, Kibo, is the highest mountain in Africa and is always snow-capped. Lower slopes are covered with dense cloud forest, a type of wet forest found only at high altitudes.*

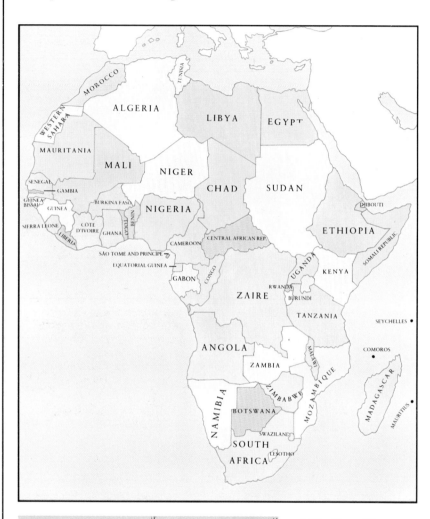

Cape Verde Islands

Praia

## AFRICAN DATAFILE

**Number of countries:** 52
**Highest point:** Kilimanjaro (Tanzania) 19,340 ft. (5,895 m)
**Lowest point:** Lake Assal (Djibouti) 5,430 ft. (1,655 m) below sea level
**Largest lake:** Victoria 224 miles (360 km) long; 26,834 sq. miles (69,500 sq. km)
**Biggest deserts:** Sahara, Kalahari, Namib
**Hottest regions:** Sahara and parts of Somalia (above 113°F/45°C)
**Longest river:** Nile (4,160 miles/6,670 km, the longest in the world)
**Other important rivers:** Zaire 2,900 miles (4,700 km); Niger 2,600 miles (4,184 km); Zambezi 2,200 miles (3,540 km)
**Greatest waterfalls:** Victoria (highest, 1,165 ft./355 m); Boyoma (most water, 2,395 ft./730 m wide)
**Largest country:** Sudan
**Most populous country:** Nigeria
**Most industrialized country:** South Africa
**Biggest city:** Cairo (Egypt) 9.8 m. people
**Other major cities (by population):** Lagos (Nigeria), Kinshasa (Zaire), Alexandria (Egypt), Casablanca (Morocco)
**Oldest civilizations:** Egypt (c.3100 B.C.), Kush (c.2000 B.C.)

◄ *The Place Djema Al Fna lies in the center of Marrakesh, the third largest city in Morocco, North Africa. Marrakesh was founded in 1062 and is one of Morocco's four traditional capital cities. A popular place for tourists to visit, this large square is always crowded with shoppers, traders, and street entertainers.*

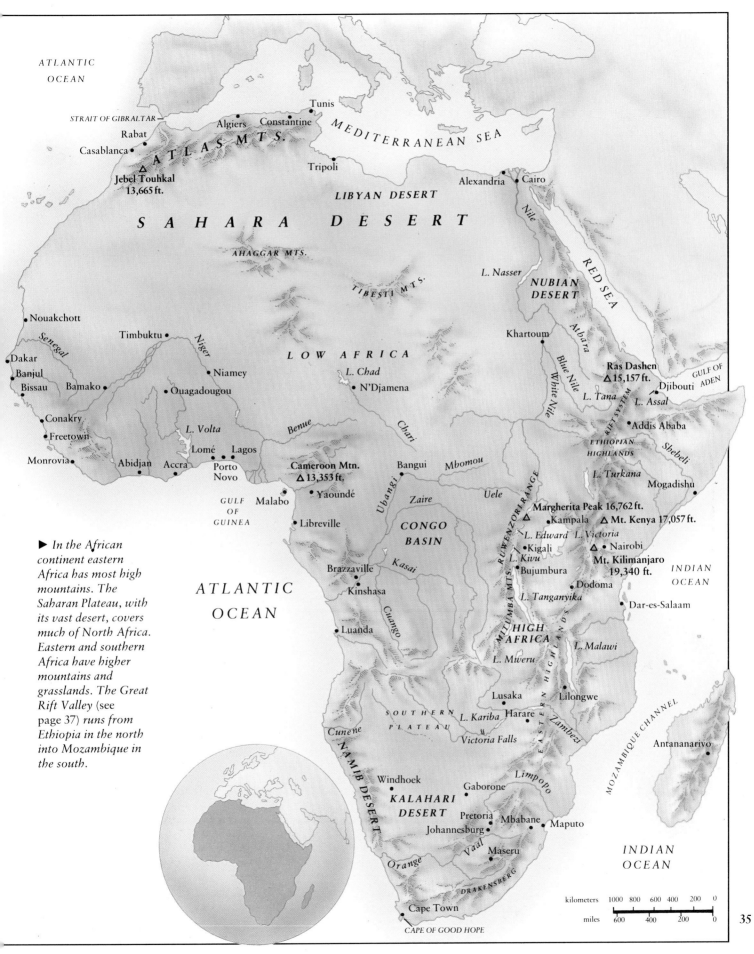

ATLANTIC
OCEAN

*STRAIT OF GIBRALTAR*

Rabat

Casablanca

△ Jebel Touhkal
13,665 ft.

Tunis

Algiers · Constantine

ATLAS MTS.

Tripoli

MEDITERRANEAN SEA

Alexandria · Cairo

LIBYAN DESERT

SAHARA DESERT

AHAGGAR MTS.

TIBESTI MTS.

L. Nasser

NUBIAN
DESERT

RED SEA

Nile

Nouakchott

Senegal

Timbuktu

Niger

LOW AFRICA

Khartoum

Atbara

Blue Nile

White Nile

Dakar
Banjul
Bissau · Bamako

Niamey

Ouagadougou

L. Chad
· N'Djamena

Ras Dashen
△ 15,157 ft.
Djibouti

GULF OF
ADEN

L. Tana

L. Assal

Conakry
· Freetown

L. Volta

Benue

Chari

Addis Ababa

Shebeli

Monrovia
Abidjan · Accra

Lomé · Lagos

Porto
Novo

Cameroon Mtn.
△ 13,353 ft.

Bangui

Mbomou

ETHIOPIAN
HIGHLANDS

L. Turkana

Mogadishu

GULF
OF
GUINEA

Malabo

· Yaoundé

· Libreville

Ubangi

Zaire

Uele

RUWENZORI RANGE

Margherita Peak 16,762 ft.
△ · Kampala

△ Mt. Kenya 17,057 ft.

CONGO
BASIN

Kasai

L. Edward L. Victoria

△ · Nairobi

ATLANTIC
OCEAN

Brazzaville

Kinshasa

· Kigali

L. Kivu
Bujumbura

Mt. Kilimanjaro
19,340 ft.

INDIAN
OCEAN

Cuango

· Luanda

HIGH
AFRICA

Dodoma

L. Tanganyika

MITUMBA MTS.

· Dar-es-Salaam

L. Mweru

L. Malawi

EASTERN HIGHLANDS

SOUTHERN
PLATEAU

Lusaka

L. Kariba Harare

Lilongwe

Zambezi

MOZAMBIQUE CHANNEL

Cunene

Victoria Falls

Antananarivo

NAMIB DESERT

Limpopo

▶ *In the African
continent eastern
Africa has most high
mountains. The
Saharan Plateau, with
its vast desert, covers
much of North Africa.
Eastern and southern
Africa have higher
mountains and
grasslands. The Great
Rift Valley (see
page 37) runs from
Ethiopia in the north
into Mozambique in
the south.*

Windhoek

Gaborone

KALAHARI
DESERT

Pretoria · Mbabane
Johannesburg · · Maputo

Vaal

Maseru

INDIAN
OCEAN

Orange

DRAKENSBERG

Cape Town

CAPE OF GOOD HOPE

kilometers 1000 800 600 400 200 0

miles 600 400 200 0

35

| COUNTRY | AREA (sq. miles) | POPULATION | CAPITAL | LANGUAGE |
|---|---|---|---|---|
| Algeria | 918,497 | 25,337,000 | Algiers | Arabic, French |
| Angola | 481,353 | 10,002,000 | Luanda | Portuguese |
| Benin | 43,483 | 4,741,000 | Porto-Novo | French |
| Botswana | 231,800 | 1,295,000 | Gaborone | Tswana, English |
| Burkina Faso | 105,869 | 9,012,000 | Ouagadougou | French |
| Burundi | 10,747 | 5,439,000 | Bujumbura | Kirundi, French |
| Cameroon | 183,568 | 11,742,000 | Yaoundé | French, English |
| Cape Verde Islands | 1,557 | 339,000 | Praia | Portuguese |
| Central African Republic | 240,534 | 2,875,000 | Bangui | French |
| Chad | 495,752 | 5,678,000 | N'Djamena | Arabic, French |
| Comoros | 838 | 463,000 | Moroni | Arabic, French |
| Congo | 132,000 | 2,236,000 | Brazzaville | French |
| Côte d'Ivoire | 124,500 | 12,657,000 | Abidjan | French |
| Djibouti | 8,500 | 528,000 | Djibouti | Arabic, French |
| Egypt | 386,650 | 53,170,000 | Cairo | Arabic, French |
| Equatorial Guinea | 10,832 | 3,511,000 | Malabo | Spanish |
| Ethiopia | 471,776 | 50,341,000 | Addis Ababa | Amharic |
| Gabon | 103,346 | 1,171,000 | Libreville | French |
| Gambia | 4,360 | 860,000 | Banjul | English |
| Ghana | 92,100 | 15,020,000 | Accra | English |
| Guinea | 94,964 | 6,876,000 | Conakry | French |
| Guinea-Bissau | 13,948 | 973,000 | Bissau | Portuguese |
| Kenya | 224,960 | 24,872,000 | Nairobi | Swahili, English |
| Lesotho | 11,720 | 1,760,000 | Maseru | Sesotho, English |
| Liberia | 43,000 | 2,595,000 | Monrovia | English |
| Libya | 679,359 | 4,206,000 | Tripoli | Arabic |
| Madagascar | 226,657 | 11,980,000 | Antananarivo | Malagasy, French |
| Malawi | 45,747 | 8,831,000 | Lilongwe | Chichewa, English |
| Mali | 478,764 | 8,152,000 | Bamako | French |
| Mauritania | 397,954 | 2,000,000 | Nouakchott | Arabic, French |
| Mauritius | 790 | 1,080,000 | Port Louis | English |
| Morocco | 172,413 | 25,113,000 | Rabat | Arabic |
| Mozambique | 303,769 | 15,696,000 | Maputo | Portuguese |

| MAJOR PRODUCTS AND INDUSTRIES | CURRENCY |
|---|---|
| Petroleum, processed foods | Dinar |
| Petroleum, vegetable and animal products | Kwanza |
| Petroleum, palm products | CFA Franc |
| Minerals, livestock products | Pula |
| Gold, manganese, millet, peanuts | CFA Franc |
| Coffee, tea, cotton | Burundi Franc |
| Petroleum, coffee, cocoa, aluminum | CFA Franc |
| Bananas, coffee, fish | Escudo |
| Coffee, diamonds, wood, cotton | CFA Franc |
| Cotton, uranium | CFA Franc |
| Vanilla, copra, perfume | Franc |
| Petroleum, wood, diamonds | CFA Franc |
| Coffee, cocoa, diamonds | CFA Franc |
| Livestock (camels), food | Djibouti Franc |
| Petroleum, cotton, textiles | Pound |
| Cocoa, timber | CFA Franc |
| Coffee, hides, livestock, pulses | Birr |
| Petroleum, timber, manganese | CFA Franc |
| Peanut products, fish, tourism | Dalasi |
| Cocoa, gold, timber | Cedi |
| Bauxite, diamonds, gold | Guinean Franc |
| Cashews, peanuts | Peso |
| Coffee, tea, petroleum products, tourism | Kenya shilling |
| Wool, foods, manufactured goods | Loti |
| Iron ore, rubber, timber | Dollar |
| Petroleum | Dinar |
| Coffee, vanilla, cloves | Franc |
| Tobacco, tea, sugar | Kwacha |
| Cotton, livestock, nuts | CFA Franc |
| Fish, iron ore | Ouguiya |
| Textiles, sugar, diamonds, fish | Rupee |
| Foods, phosphates, fertilizer | Dirham |
| Shrimps, cashews, cotton, sugar | Metical |

## COLONIAL PARTITIONING OF AFRICA

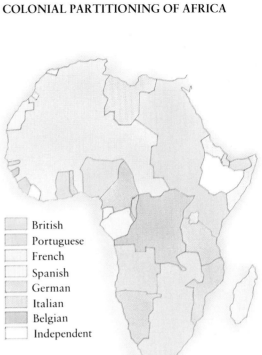

British
Portuguese
French
Spanish
German
Italian
Belgian
Independent

By the end of the 1800s, most of Africa was shared out between the European powers. The map of Africa was drawn by empire-builders, and colonial frontier lines have shaped the boundaries of the independent nations of modern Africa. As a result, national boundaries cut across the homelands of the more than 800 different ethnic groups of African people.

### THE GREAT RIFT VALLEY
The Rift Valley is a series of cracks in the Earth's surface, running 4,040 miles (6,500 km) from East Africa to Asia. In the steep-sided rift valleys lie rich farmland and Africa's great lakes.

GREAT
RIFT
VALLEY

| COUNTRY | AREA (sq. miles) | POPULATION | CAPITAL | LANGUAGE |
|---|---|---|---|---|
| Namibia | 317,818 | 1,302,000 | Windhoek | Afrikaans, English |
| Niger | 489,189 | 7,779,000 | Niamey | French, Hausa |
| Nigeria | 356,667 | 119,812,000 | Lagos/Abuja* | English |
| Rwanda | 10,169 | 7,232,000 | Kigali | Kinyarwanda, French |
| São Tomé & Príncipe | 372 | 121,000 | São Tomé | Portuguese |
| Senegal | 75,750 | 7,317,000 | Dakar | French |
| Seychelles | 108 | 68,700 | Victoria | Creole, English, French |
| Sierra Leone | 27,700 | 4,151,000 | Freetown | English |
| Somalia | 246,300 | 7,555,000 | Mogadishu | Somali, Arabic |
| South Africa | 472,360 | 37,419,000 | Pretoria | Afrikaans, English |
| Sudan | 966,757 | 28,311,000 | Khartoum | Arabic |
| Swaziland | 6,704 | 770,000 | Mbabane | Swazi, English |
| Tanzania | 364,886 | 24,403,000 | Dodoma | Swahili, English |
| Togo | 21,622 | 3,764,000 | Lomé | French |
| Tunisia | 63,170 | 8,182,000 | Tunis | Arabic |
| Uganda | 93,354 | 16,928,000 | Kampala | Swahili, English |
| Zaire | 905,563 | 34,138,000 | Kinshasa | French |
| Zambia | 290,586 | 8,456,000 | Lusaka | English |
| Zimbabwe | 150,803 | 9,369,000 | Harare | English |

▶ *The Sahara Desert has both the world's highest temperatures and the biggest sand dunes; some dunes are 1,300 ft. (400 m) high.*

▼ *The Pyramids at Giza in Egypt built c.2500s B.C. Of the Seven Wonders of the Ancient World, only the Pyramids survive.*

▶ *The legislative capital of South Africa, Cape Town, is a bustling trading and shipping center on the southwest coast of Africa. The famous Table Mountain towers over the city and its harbor.*

| MAJOR PRODUCTS AND INDUSTRIES | CURRENCY |
|---|---|
| Diamonds, cattle, hides | Rand |
| Uranium, other minerals, livestock, vegetables | CFA Franc |
| Petroleum, palm products | Naira |
| Coffee, tea | Rwanda Franc |
| Cocoa, copra | Dobre |
| Peanut oil, shellfish, phosphates | CFA Franc |
| Petroleum, fish, tourism | S Rupee |
| Titanium dioxide, diamonds, bauxite, coffee | Leone |
| Livestock, bananas, hides, fish | Somali Shilling |
| Gold, minerals, foods, factory goods | Rand |
| Cotton, gum arabic, sesame, sheep | Sudanese Pound |
| Sugar, timber, coal, diamonds | Lilangeni |
| Coffee, cotton | Tanzanian Shilling |
| Fertilizer, coffee, tea, cocoa | CFA Franc |
| Clothing, petroleum, phosphates | Dinar |
| Coffee | Uganda Shilling |
| Copper, coffee, diamonds, petroleum | Zaire |
| Copper, zinc, cobalt | Kwacha |
| Tobacco, gold | Zimbabwe dollar |

▲ *The Zaïre River, formerly known as the Congo, in west-central Africa is 2,900 miles (4,667 km) long. Although it is an important transportation route, rapids prevent upper river navigation.*

▼ *Muslims in Nigeria celebrate the end of Ramadan, the holy month of fasting. About half of Nigeria's population are Muslim, with some 40 percent Christian. Other Nigerians practice traditional religions.*

◄ *The Nile River, the longest river in the world, has always been the lifeblood of Egypt. Its waters made farming possible in an area of desert.*

▼ *The Great Mosque at Djenne in Mali, West Africa is a modern example (1907) of traditional building; it is built of sun-dried mud bricks.*

▼ The Cullinan *is the largest diamond ever mined; it is 3,106 carats and was found in South Africa in 1905.*

# Oceania

Oceania is actually mostly water—the Pacific Ocean. By far the biggest landmass in Oceania is Australia, sometimes considered a continent in its own right. Much of Australia is empty desert. Next in size are Papua New Guinea and New Zealand. Scattered across the wide Pacific Ocean are about 30,000 islands. These islands form three main groups: Melanesia, Micronesia, and Polynesia. The people of Oceania are mostly descendants of migrants who originally came from Asia or Europe.

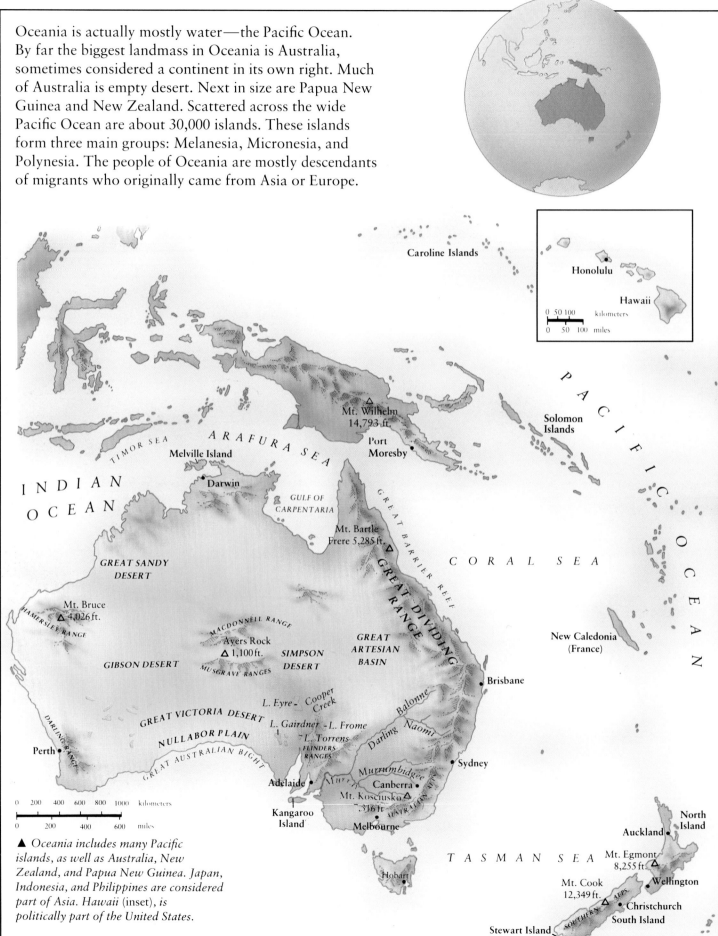

Honolulu

Hawaii

0  50 100  kilometers
0  50  100  miles

Caroline Islands

PACIFIC OCEAN

Mt. Wilhelm 14,793 ft.

Solomon Islands

Port Moresby

ARAFURA SEA

TIMOR SEA

Melville Island

Darwin

GULF OF CARPENTARIA

Mt. Bartle Frere 5,285 ft.

GREAT BARRIER REEF

CORAL SEA

INDIAN OCEAN

GREAT SANDY DESERT

Mt. Bruce 4,026 ft.

HAMERSLEY RANGE

MACDONNELL RANGE

Ayers Rock 1,100 ft.

SIMPSON DESERT

GREAT DIVIDING RANGE

GREAT ARTESIAN BASIN

New Caledonia (France)

GIBSON DESERT

MUSGRAVE RANGES

Brisbane

GREAT VICTORIA DESERT

L. Eyre

Cooper Creek

Balonne

DARLING RANGE

NULLARBOR PLAIN

L. Gairdner

L. Frome

L. Torrens

FLINDERS RANGES

Darling

Naomi

Perth

GREAT AUSTRALIAN BIGHT

Murrumbidgee

Sydney

Adelaide

Murray

Canberra

AUSTRALIAN ALPS

Mt. Kosciusko 7,316 ft.

North Island

Kangaroo Island

Melbourne

Auckland

0  200  400  800  1000  kilometers
0  200  400  600  miles

TASMAN SEA

Mt. Egmont 8,255 ft.

Wellington

Hobart

Mt. Cook 12,349 ft.

SOUTHERN ALPS

Christchurch

South Island

Stewart Island

▲ Oceania includes many Pacific islands, as well as Australia, New Zealand, and Papua New Guinea. Japan, Indonesia, and Philippines are considered part of Asia. Hawaii (inset), is politically part of the United States.

40

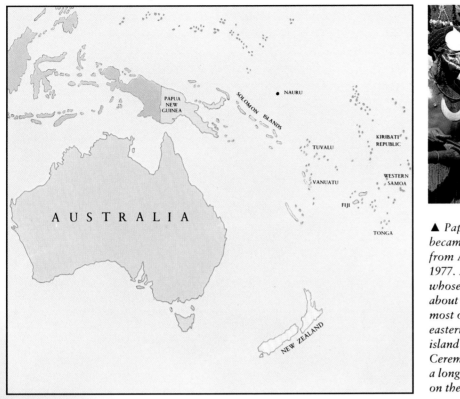

▲ *Papua New Guinea became independent from Australia in 1977. A country whose people speak about 700 languages, most of it occupies the eastern part of the island of New Guinea. Ceremonial dances are a longtime tradition on the islands.*

▼ *Australia's second largest city, Melbourne, is a busy port and financial center on the southeastern coast. Due to substantial postwar industrial growth, the city's population now includes people of Greek, Italian, Chinese, and British origin.*

Samoan
Islands

an Islands

### OCEANIAC DATAFILE

**Number of countries:** 11
**Biggest desert:** Australian Desert (includes several deserts totaling over 500,000 sq. miles 1.5 million sq. km)
**Highest mountain:** Mt. Wilhelm, Papua New Guinea, 14,793 ft. (4,509 m)
**Longest permanently flowing river:** Murray (Australia), 1,600 miles (2,575 km)
**Largest country:** Australia
**Largest city (by population):** Sydney (Australia). Other major cities: Melbourne, Adelaide, Perth, Brisbane, Hobart (all in Australia); Wellington, Auckland (both in New Zealand)

◄ *The British established six colonies in Australia from 1788–1859. When Australia became independent (1901) the colonies became states.*

► *The North Island of New Zealand has active volcanoes, spouting geysers, and a region of bubbling hot thermal springs.*

| COUNTRY | AREA (sq. miles) | POPULATION | CAPITAL | LANGUAGES |
|---|---|---|---|---|
| Australia | 2,966,200 | 17,073,000 | Canberra | English |
| Fiji | 7,055 | 740,000 | Suva | English, Fijian, Hindi |
| Kiribati | 266 | 71,000 | Bairiki | English, I-Kiribati |
| Nauru | 8 | 9300 | Domaneab | Nauruan, English |
| New Zealand | 103,736 | 3,390,000 | Wellington | English |
| Papua New Guinea | 178,260 | 3,671,000 | Port Moresby | English, local languages |
| Solomon Islands | 10,640 | 319,000 | Honiara | English, Pidgin |
| Tonga | 270 | 96,300 | Nuku'alofa | Tongan, English |
| Tuvalu | 10 | 9100 | Fongafale | Tuvaluan, English |
| Vanuatu | 5,700 | 147,000 | Vila | Bislama, English, French |
| Western Samoa | 1,133 | 165,000 | Apia | Samoan, English |

◀ A view of Sydney Harbour, Australia. The famous 1970s opera house (center) confronts a steel arch bridge built in 1932.

▼ Ayers Rock in central Australia is an enormous solitary rock, 1,100 ft. (335 m) high and 6 miles (10 km) around its base.

**THE GREAT BARRIER REEF**
The world's longest reef, 1,260 miles (2,027 km) long, is off the coast of Queensland, Australia. It is the biggest structure ever made by living creatures, and contains 350 different corals. The Great Barrier Reef is actually a chain of more than 2,500 reefs and islands.

◀ Much of Australia is too dry for crop-raising, but is suitable for sheep-rearing. The world's longest fence is in Queensland. Its 3,400 miles (5,500 km) of wire was put up to protect sheep from attacks by dingos (wild dogs).

| MAJOR PRODUCTS AND INDUSTRIES | CURRENCY |
| --- | --- |
| Minerals, machinery, foods, wool | Australian Dollar |
| Sugar, copra, fish, timber | Fiji Dollar |
| Copra, fish | Australian Dollar |
| Phosphates, financial services | Australian Dollar |
| Dairy foods, lamb, wool, fish | N. Zealand Dollar |
| Copper, coffee, timber | Kina |
| Copra, cocoa, coconuts | Solomon Is. Dollar |
| Vanilla, vegetables, fish, coconuts | Pa'anga |
| Copra | Tuvalu Dollar |
| Copra, meat, cocoa, timber | Vatu |
| Coconut products, taro, timber | Tala |

## THE PACIFIC ISLANDS

It is estimated that there are between 20,000 and 30,000 islands in the Pacific Ocean. Easter Island is a remote speck of land 2,360 miles (3,800 km) west of Chile in South America, from where the people who made its strange stone figures *(below)* probably came. Its population is about 2,000.

▲ *A fruit farm on Vitu Levu, or "Great Fiji," the largest of 844 islands that make up the South Pacific state of Fiji. Only about 100 Fijian islands are inhabited.*

▼ *Fjordland is a region of spectacular scenery along the southwest coast of South Island, New Zealand. The fjords are long inlets cut into the land.*

# Antarctica

Antarctica is larger than either Europe or Australia. It is a landmass, but it lies buried beneath a massive icecap, which is on average about 6,000 ft. (2,000 m) thick. Ice and snow cover 98 percent of Antarctica. Only a few mountains and rocky areas show above the icecap. A small number of plants, insects, and animals live on the mainland, but Antarctica has no permanent human population, although scientists work at research bases. The geographic South Pole is near the center of Antarctica, on a high, windy plateau.

### ANTARCTIC DATAFILE

**Number of countries:** None, but several countries claim sectors of the continent
**Area:** About 5,000,000 sq. miles (14,000,000 sq. km)
**Highest point:** Vinson Massif 16,860 ft. (5,140 m)
**Ice:** The ice sheet has a volume of about 12 m sq. miles (30 m sq. km); deepest part is about 15,750 ft. (4,800 m)
**Biggest glaciers:** Amundsen, Beardmore, Lambert (world's longest), Scott
**Snowfall:** About 25 in. (60 cm) a year at the coast, only 2 in. (5 cm) a year on the plateau
**Lowest temperature:** −128.5°F (−89.2°C) at Vostok Research Base, 1983

◀ *Antarctica is a continent buried beneath an immense ice sheet. Exploration of this barren landmass did not begin until the 1900s.*

ATLANTIC OCEAN

QUEEN MAUD LAND

MÜHLING HOFFMANN MTS.

BELLINGSHAUSEN SEA

ANTARCTIC PENINSULA

LARSEN ICE SHELF

WEDDELL SEA

COATS LAND

Molodezhnaya Research Base

ENDERBY LAND

PALMER LAND

EDITH RONNE ICE SHELF

ABBOT ICE SHELF

ELLSWORTH LAND

Vinson Massif 16,860 ft.

PRINCE CHARLES MTS.

Mt. Menzies 11,007 ft.

Lambert Glacier

AMERY ICE SHELF

WEST ANTARCTICA

Amundsen-Scott Research Base

South Pole

ELLSWORTH MTS.

TRANSANTARCTIC MTS.

EAST ANTARCTICA

INDIAN OCEAN

AMUNDSEN SEA

BYRD LAND

WEST ICE SHELF

Mt. Kirkpatrick 14,856 ft.

ROSS ICE SHELF

Mt. Markham 14,275 ft.

Vostok Research Base

Mt. Erebus 12,447 ft.

SHACKLETON ICE SHELF

PACIFIC OCEAN

ROSS SEA

VICTORIA LAND

Casey Research Base

WILKES LAND

| kilometers | 0 | 200 | 400 | 600 | 800 | 1000 |
| miles | 0 | | 200 | 400 | | 600 |

▲ An iceberg dwarfs a fishing boat. The biggest iceberg ever seen covered 11,970 sq. miles (31,000 sq. km).

▶ A colony of King penguins in the Antarctic. These flightless birds are the continent's largest non-human inhabitants.

▲ Mt. Erebus on Ross Island is Antarctica's largest active volcano. From time to time it spews up volcanic rock. Its peak is 12,447 ft. (3,794 m) high.

▼ This member of the British Antarctic Survey is one of many scientists trying to protect Antarctica and the wildlife on its coasts from exploitation.

### EXPLORING ANTARCTICA

European sailors first sighted Antarctica in the early 1800s. In 1911 Roald Amundsen of Norway led the first explorers to the South Pole, beating a British expedition led by Robert F. Scott by five weeks. Scott and his men all died on the return journey. In 1929, Richard Byrd of the U.S. Navy flew over the South Pole for the first time. In 1957–1958 a British Commonwealth expedition, led by the British geologist Vivian Fuchs, made the first overland crossing of the continent.

▲ Amundsen's party reached the South Pole in December 1911. Using skis and dog sleds, all the men returned safely.

# Countries

In the past, the boundaries of a people's territory were set either by natural barriers such as rivers or mountains, or by the power of its ruler. The idea of the nation-state, of people united by common laws, languages, and customs, developed only gradually. But nationalism is a powerful and sometimes dangerous idea: it fired the American Revolution and created new European countries in the 1800s. States are still being made and unmade. As people shift allegiances, the world map is once again redrawn.

## THE ROMAN WORLD
The Roman Empire at its peak covered much of Europe, North Africa, and the Mediterranean. Rome was the heart of an empire which included a number of tribes and kingdoms, first by conquest and then by the imposition of Roman law. There were no countries within the Roman Empire, only peoples.

▼ Countries break records in many ways. Some are very big, with many millions of inhabitants: at over 6.5 million sq. miles (17 million sq. km), Russia is easily the world's biggest country by area, while China has by far the most people. Other countries get into the record books because they are tiny: Monaco, on the coast of southern France, has an area of only 0.7 sq. miles (1.9 sq. km).

## TEN SMALLEST COUNTRIES

| 1 Vatican City State | 108.7 acres |
|---|---|
| 2 Monaco | 0.7 sq. miles |
| 3 Nauru | 8 sq. miles |
| 4 Tuvalu | 10 sq. miles |
| 5 San Marino | 24 sq. miles |
| 6 Liechtenstein | 62 sq. miles |
| 7 St. Kitts-Nevis | 101 sq. miles |
| 8 Maldives | 115 sq. miles |
| 9 Malta | 122 sq. miles |
| 10 Grenada | 133 sq. miles |

## TEN LARGEST COUNTRIES

| 1 Russia | 6,592,818 sq. miles |
|---|---|
| 2 Canada | 3,849,000 sq. miles |
| 3 China | 3,696,100 sq. miles |
| 4 U.S.A. | 3,618,770 sq. miles |
| 5 Brazil | 3,286,470 sq. miles |
| 6 Australia | 2,967,200 sq. miles |
| 7 India | 1,266,595 sq. miles |
| 8 Argentina | 1,065,189 sq. miles |
| 9 Sudan | 966,757 sq. miles |
| 10 Algeria | 918,497 sq. miles |

### THE AMERICAS
1 BELIZE
2 HONDURAS
3 NICARAGUA
4 GUATEMALA
5 EL SALVADOR
6 COSTA RICA
7 PANAMA
8 HAITI
9 DOMINICAN REPUBLIC
10 PUERTO RICO
11 GUYANA
12 SURINAM
13 FRENCH GUIANA
14 PARAGUAY
15 URUGUAY
16 ECUADOR

► This map shows the world today. Political borders and country names can change dramatically, as happened when the Soviet Union broke up in the early 1990s.

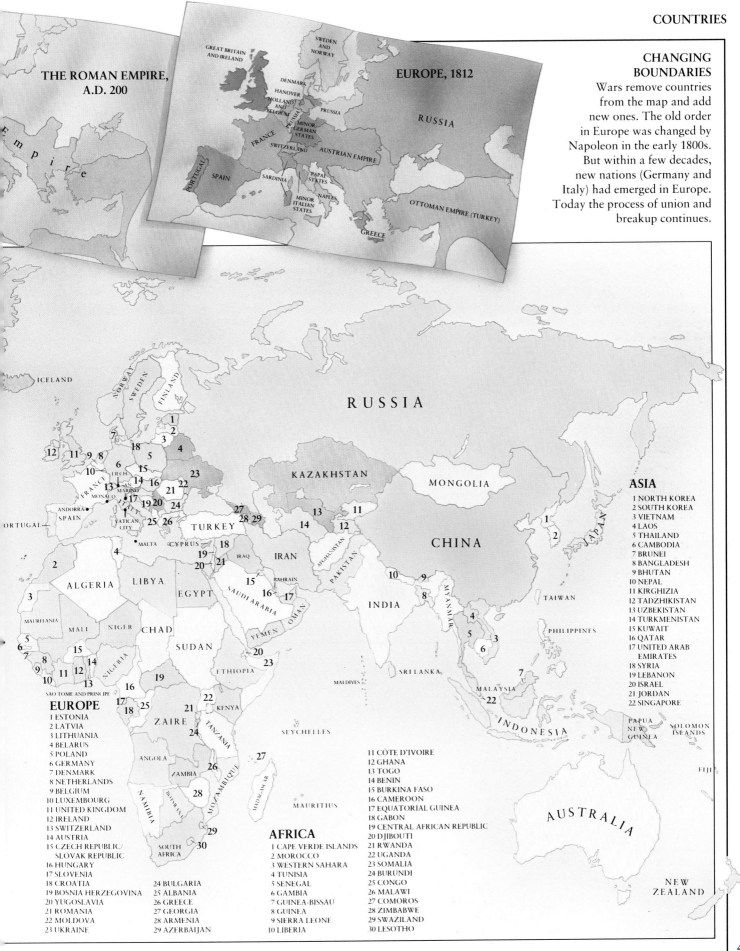

## THE ROMAN EMPIRE, A.D. 200

*Empire*

## EUROPE, 1812

GREAT BRITAIN AND IRELAND
SWEDEN AND NORWAY
DENMARK
HANOVER
HOLLAND AND BELGIUM
PRUSSIA
MINOR GERMAN STATES
FRANCE
RUSSIA
SWITZERLAND
AUSTRIAN EMPIRE
PORTUGAL
SPAIN
SARDINIA
PAPAL STATES
MINOR ITALIAN STATES
NAPLES
OTTOMAN EMPIRE (TURKEY)
GREECE

## CHANGING BOUNDARIES

Wars remove countries from the map and add new ones. The old order in Europe was changed by Napoleon in the early 1800s. But within a few decades, new nations (Germany and Italy) had emerged in Europe. Today the process of union and breakup continues.

### EUROPE
1 ESTONIA
2 LATVIA
3 LITHUANIA
4 BELARUS
5 POLAND
6 GERMANY
7 DENMARK
8 NETHERLANDS
9 BELGIUM
10 LUXEMBOURG
11 UNITED KINGDOM
12 IRELAND
13 SWITZERLAND
14 AUSTRIA
15 CZECH REPUBLIC/ SLOVAK REPUBLIC
16 HUNGARY
17 SLOVENIA
18 CROATIA
19 BOSNIA HERZEGOVINA
20 YUGOSLAVIA
21 ROMANIA
22 MOLDOVA
23 UKRAINE
24 BULGARIA
25 ALBANIA
26 GREECE
27 GEORGIA
28 ARMENIA
29 AZERBAIJAN

### AFRICA
1 CAPE VERDE ISLANDS
2 MOROCCO
3 WESTERN SAHARA
4 TUNISIA
5 SENEGAL
6 GAMBIA
7 GUINEA-BISSAU
8 GUINEA
9 SIERRA LEONE
10 LIBERIA
11 CÔTE D'IVOIRE
12 GHANA
13 TOGO
14 BENIN
15 BURKINA FASO
16 CAMEROON
17 EQUATORIAL GUINEA
18 GABON
19 CENTRAL AFRICAN REPUBLIC
20 DJIBOUTI
21 RWANDA
22 UGANDA
23 SOMALIA
24 BURUNDI
25 CONGO
26 MALAWI
27 COMOROS
28 ZIMBABWE
29 SWAZILAND
30 LESOTHO

### ASIA
1 NORTH KOREA
2 SOUTH KOREA
3 VIETNAM
4 LAOS
5 THAILAND
6 CAMBODIA
7 BRUNEI
8 BANGLADESH
9 BHUTAN
10 NEPAL
11 KIRGHIZIA
12 TADZHIKISTAN
13 UZBEKISTAN
14 TURKMENISTAN
15 KUWAIT
16 QATAR
17 UNITED ARAB EMIRATES
18 SYRIA
19 LEBANON
20 ISRAEL
21 JORDAN
22 SINGAPORE

# CULTURES

## Population

Culture embraces many aspects of human life: art, religion, customs, language, technology. Cultures are amazingly diverse, even though in the 20th century "world culture" (that is, western industrial culture) has touched almost every human group from the Amazon to the Arctic. Every year there are about 90 million extra people to share that culture. The human population grew slowly until the 1800s, since when the rate of increase has quickened dramatically. However, population growth is not the same worldwide. In the more prosperous countries, birth rates roughly match the numbers of deaths, so that populations stay stable or grow only slowly. In developing countries, birth rates far outstrip death rates, and consequently many of these countries have populations growing at two to three percent a year.

**POPULATION DISTRIBUTION**

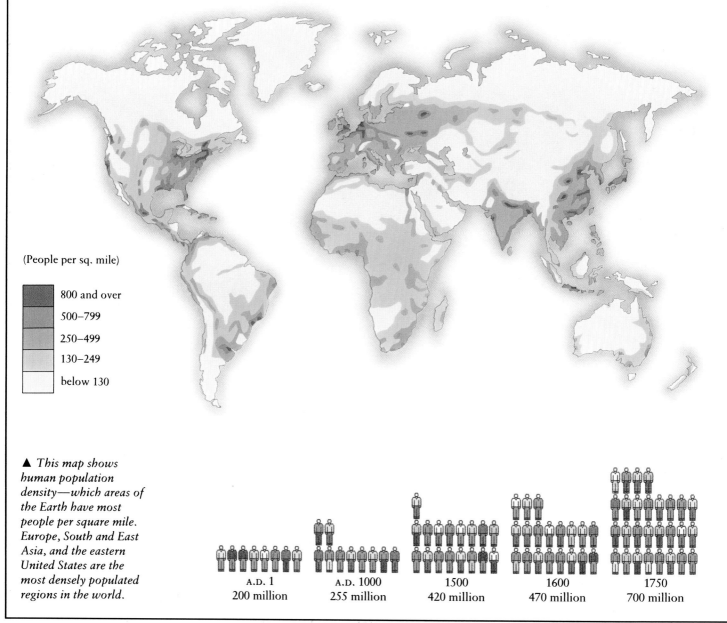

(People per sq. mile)

800 and over
500–799
250–499
130–249
below 130

▲ *This map shows human population density—which areas of the Earth have most people per square mile. Europe, South and East Asia, and the eastern United States are the most densely populated regions in the world.*

A.D. 1
200 million

A.D. 1000
255 million

1500
420 million

1600
470 million

1750
700 million

## ANNUAL RATES OF INCREASE

| | |
|---|---|
| World | 1.7% |
| Africa | 3.0% |
| South America | 1.9% |
| Asia | 1.8% |
| Oceania | 1.4% |
| North America | 1.2% |
| Europe | 0.2% |

The world's population is rising fastest in the so-called developing world, particularly in Africa. In Kenya the population doubles every 18 to 23 years. But in some Western countries (Sweden, for example) the population is actually falling.

**POPULATION DISTRIBUTION** (Right)
Of the seven continents, Asia has by far the most people. Nearly six out of ten people live in Asia. Between them China and India have nearly 40 percent of all the world's people.

**POPULATION EXPLOSION** (Below)
The growth of human population was slow until the 1700s. It doubled from the mid-1600s to 1850, and has more than quadrupled since then. In 1950 the Earth's population was about 2.5 billion. In the year 2000 it will be over six billion.

= 25 million people

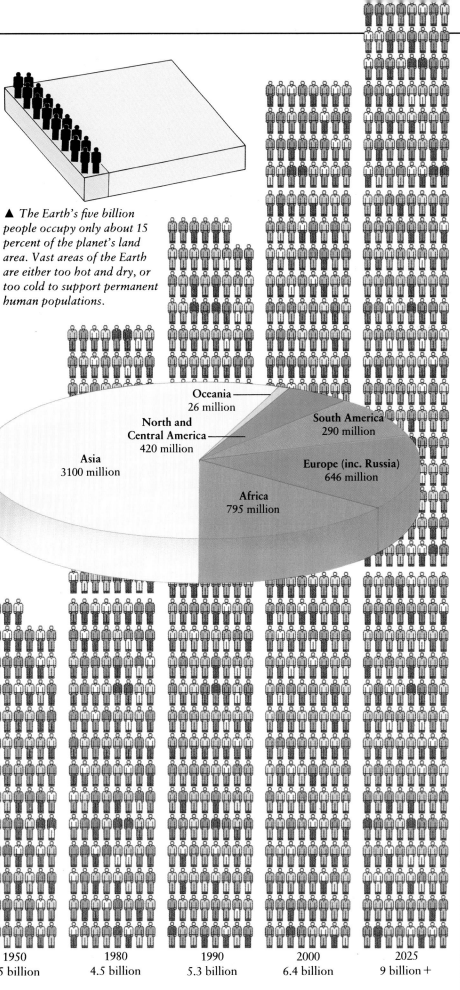

▲ The Earth's five billion people occupy only about 15 percent of the planet's land area. Vast areas of the Earth are either too hot and dry, or too cold to support permanent human populations.

**Oceania** 26 million
**North and Central America** 420 million
**South America** 290 million
**Asia** 3100 million
**Europe (inc. Russia)** 646 million
**Africa** 795 million

| 1850 | 1900 | 1950 | 1980 | 1990 | 2000 | 2025 |
|---|---|---|---|---|---|---|
| 1.2 billion | 1.6 billion | 2.5 billion | 4.5 billion | 5.3 billion | 6.4 billion | 9 billion + |

# Cities

In 1800 no more than one in every 20 people lived in a city. Most people lived in villages. City growth accelerated in the 1800s and today 8 in 20 people are city-dwellers. By the 2000s there will be more people living in towns and cities than in the countryside. People moving into towns in large numbers causes problems of inadequate housing, transportation, food supply, public health, and employment. In the developing countries in particular, there are insufficient resources to cope with these problems.

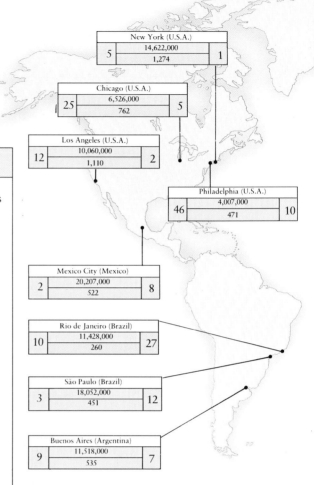

| New York (U.S.A.) | | |
|---|---|---|
| 5 | 14,622,000 | 1 |
| | 1,274 | |

| Chicago (U.S.A.) | | |
|---|---|---|
| 25 | 6,526,000 | 5 |
| | 762 | |

| Los Angeles (U.S.A.) | | |
|---|---|---|
| 12 | 10,060,000 | 2 |
| | 1,110 | |

| Philadelphia (U.S.A.) | | |
|---|---|---|
| 46 | 4,007,000 | 10 |
| | 471 | |

| Mexico City (Mexico) | | |
|---|---|---|
| 2 | 20,207,000 | 8 |
| | 522 | |

| Rio de Janeiro (Brazil) | | |
|---|---|---|
| 10 | 11,428,000 | 27 |
| | 260 | |

| São Paulo (Brazil) | | |
|---|---|---|
| 3 | 18,052,000 | 12 |
| | 451 | |

| Buenos Aires (Argentina) | | |
|---|---|---|
| 9 | 11,518,000 | 7 |
| | 535 | |

## FACTS ABOUT CITIES

• The world's oldest capital city is Damascus in Syria. It has been inhabited for about 4,500 years.

• In 1800 less than three percent of the world's population lived in towns and cities. By the year 2000 it is expected that 50 percent of the world's population will live in cities or large towns.

• Cities grew rapidly in Europe and North America in the 1800s, during the Industrial Revolution. For example, Chicago grew from a town of 4,000 people in 1840 to a booming city of more than one million inhabitants in 1890.

• Fires and earthquakes have devastated even the greatest cities. London's Great Fire of 1666 burned for six days. In 1906 an earthquake shook San Francisco. Fires broke out, more than 28,000 buildings were destroyed, and about 3,000 people died.

• Tokyo-Yokohama in Japan and Mexico City in Mexico rank as the two biggest urban areas in the world. Both have populations of more than 20 million people.

• India has two of the world's fastest-growing cities. By the year 2000 Calcutta and Bombay will probably rank fourth and fifth in the world, each topping 16 million people.

• Where are a city's limits? This is not always easy to say. Some city limits are fixed so they do not overlap neighboring towns. Others include such towns, creating much larger metropolitan areas.

• Africa's biggest cities include Cairo (Egypt) 9.8 million people; Lagos (Nigeria), Alexandria (Egypt), Kinshasa (Zaïre), and Casablanca (Morocco) all have populations of over 2 million people.

• The biggest city in Australia is Sydney (about 3 million people).

• São Paulo, Brazil, is South America's largest city. Its metropolitan population is over 12.5 million.

▶ *Fast city growth often causes acute housing shortages. The self-built shacks in the* favelas *(slums) provide shelter for poor people on the hillsides around Rio de Janeiro in Brazil.*

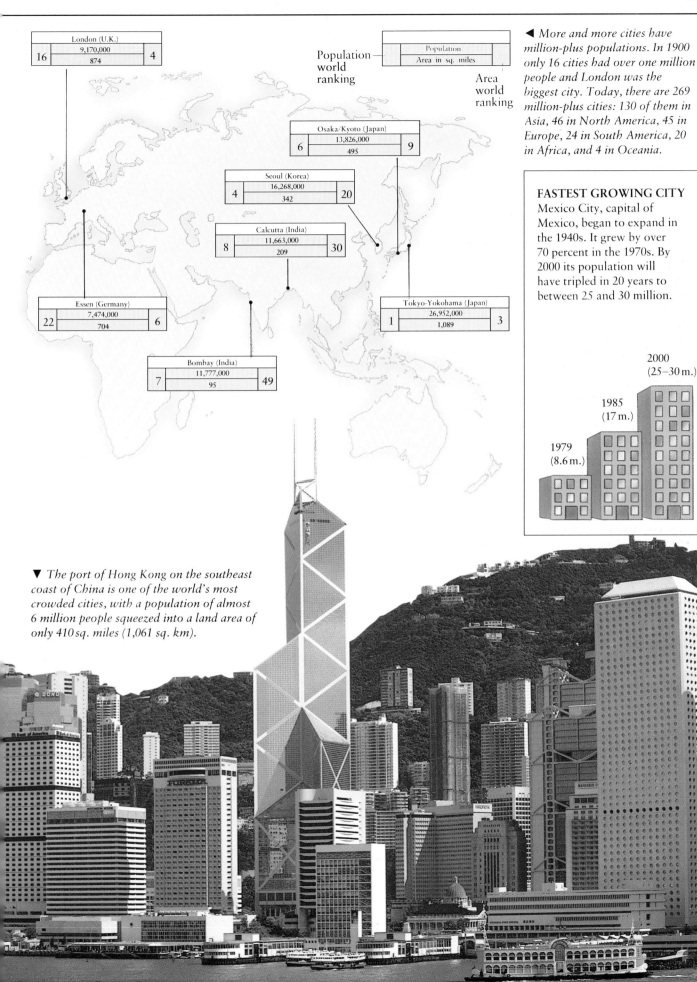

London (U.K.)

| 16 | 9,170,000 | 4 |
| --- | --- | --- |
| | 874 | |

Population world ranking

| | Population | |
| --- | --- | --- |
| | Area in sq. miles | |

Area world ranking

Osaka/Kyoto (Japan)

| 6 | 13,826,000 | 9 |
| --- | --- | --- |
| | 495 | |

Seoul (Korea)

| 4 | 16,268,000 | 20 |
| --- | --- | --- |
| | 342 | |

Calcutta (India)

| 8 | 11,663,000 | 30 |
| --- | --- | --- |
| | 209 | |

Essen (Germany)

| 22 | 7,474,000 | 6 |
| --- | --- | --- |
| | 704 | |

Tokyo-Yokohama (Japan)

| 1 | 26,952,000 | 3 |
| --- | --- | --- |
| | 1,089 | |

Bombay (India)

| 7 | 11,777,000 | 49 |
| --- | --- | --- |
| | 95 | |

◀ *More and more cities have million-plus populations. In 1900 only 16 cities had over one million people and London was the biggest city. Today, there are 269 million-plus cities: 130 of them in Asia, 46 in North America, 45 in Europe, 24 in South America, 20 in Africa, and 4 in Oceania.*

**FASTEST GROWING CITY**
Mexico City, capital of Mexico, began to expand in the 1940s. It grew by over 70 percent in the 1970s. By 2000 its population will have tripled in 20 years to between 25 and 30 million.

2000
(25–30 m.)

1985
(17 m.)

1979
(8.6 m.)

▼ *The port of Hong Kong on the southeast coast of China is one of the world's most crowded cities, with a population of almost 6 million people squeezed into a land area of only 410 sq. miles (1,061 sq. km).*

# Peoples

We all belong to the same species, *Homo sapiens sapiens*. Over many thousands of years, people living in different parts of the Earth developed different characteristics. Groups of people that share the same characteristics belong to the same race. Their physical features are the result of heredity, the passing on of resemblances from parents to children through genetic inheritance. So members of a racial group are "related" biologically in the same way as members of a family group are related.

**FACTS ABOUT PEOPLES**

● People of the same race share certain physical characteristics such as hair type. Less obvious are differences in blood groups (few Australian Aborigines have type B blood, common in Africa and Asia).
● Almost all West African people have third molar or wisdom teeth, but many people of Asian origin do not have these teeth.

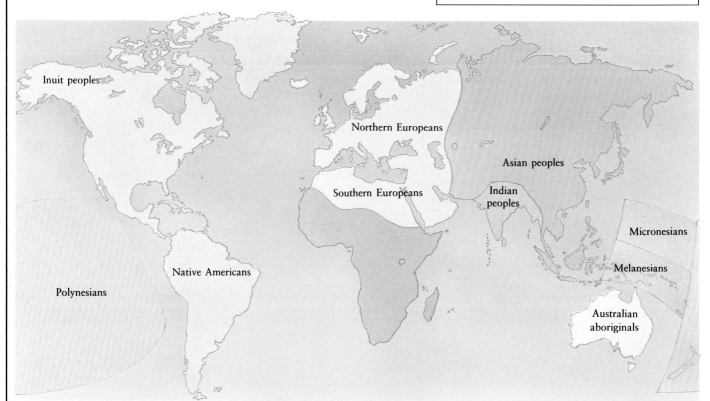

▲ *This map shows the areas of the world where the main geographical races lived before the 1500s. They developed in comparative isolation, separated from one another by oceans, mountains, and deserts.*

▶ *From the 1500s on, overseas exploration and mass migration altered the population map. For example, about half as many people of European descent now live outside Europe as in Europe. Arrows show major migrations.*

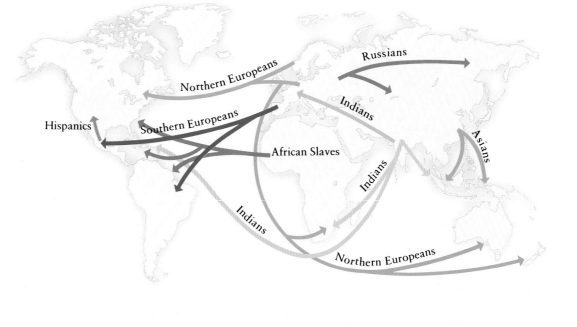

## HUMAN VARIATION
The United States' racial blend is the result of thousands of years of migration, colonization, and slavery. On streets in cities such as New York you can see a varied population of predominantly English-speaking Americans whose ancestors came from Europe, Asia, South and Central America, Africa, and the Pacific and Caribbean islands.

## WORLDWIDE AGE DISTRIBUTION
In the developing world (countries in Africa and Asia), an average of about 37 percent of the total population is made up of children under 15 years old. However, in some African countries, the proportion of children is even higher—about 45 percent of the total population. This figure is based on the calculation that the average woman in Africa has more than 6 children.

### LIFE EXPECTANCY (1989)

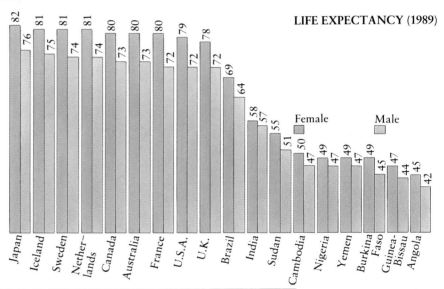

| | Female | Male |
|---|---|---|
| Japan | 82 | 76 |
| Iceland | 81 | 75 |
| Sweden | 81 | 74 |
| Netherlands | 81 | 74 |
| Canada | 80 | 73 |
| Australia | 80 | 73 |
| France | 80 | 72 |
| U.S.A. | 79 | 72 |
| U.K. | 78 | 72 |
| Brazil | 69 | 64 |
| India | 58 | 57 |
| Sudan | 55 | 51 |
| Cambodia | 50 | 47 |
| Nigeria | 49 | 47 |
| Yemen | 49 | 47 |
| Burkina Faso | 49 | 45 |
| Guinea-Bissau | 47 | 44 |
| Angola | 45 | 42 |

### DEVELOPING COUNTRY

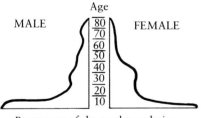

MALE — Age — FEMALE

80 70 60 50 40 30 20 10

Percentage of the total population

### DEVELOPED COUNTRY

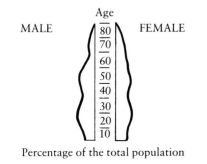

MALE — Age — FEMALE

80 70 60 50 40 30 20 10

Percentage of the total population

▲ People generally are living longer but life expectancy varies greatly. Women everywhere live longer than men. The deaths of infants and of mothers in childbirth partly explain the difference between the developed and developing countries.

◄ In the developing world, health workers in clinics (here administering vaccinations in Bangladesh) can cut child mortality rates, combat malnutrition, and check disease.

# Language

The world's people speak between 4,000 and 5,000 languages and dialects (local variations of a language). About 845 of these languages are spoken in India. The language spoken by the greatest number of people in the world is Mandarin Chinese. English is the most widely spoken language. All languages change so long as people speak them. New words are added, others fall out of use. In a few hundred years, a language can become totally different. A language no longer spoken is called dead.

## MAJOR LANGUAGE GROUPS

### FACTS ABOUT LANGUAGE

- Korean appears to be unrelated to any other language.
- Papua New Guinea has a remarkably large number of languages—over 700.
- Every language has the vowel sound "a," as pronounced in the English word "father."
- Many words change languages. For example, English has borrowed planet (Greek), video (Latin), algebra (Arabic), chocolate (Native American), thug (Hindi), and knife (Norse) among others.

▼ *Most Canadians speak English, but in Quebec, where 95 percent of the people have French ancestors, French is usually spoken.*

Indo-European
Sino-Tibetan
Black African
Malayo-Polynesian
Afro-Asian
Dravidian
Japanese and Korean
Uralic and Altaic
Mon-Khmer
Other Languages

▲ *This map shows the chief language groups and where they are most widely spoken. Almost half the world's peoples speak Indo-European languages. This group originated among peoples living in the area from northern India to Europe.*

## LANGUAGE FAMILIES

All languages within a family have developed from an original parent language. Indo-European has eight groups or branches, shown in the "family tree" (right). English belongs to the Germanic branch, which also includes German, Dutch, and the Scandinavian languages. Other language branches, such as Albanian, have no offshoots.

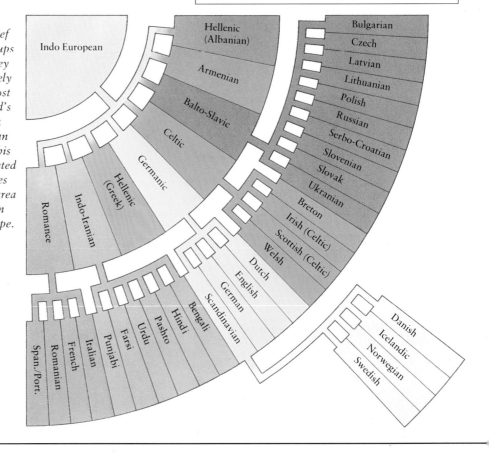

Indo European

Hellenic (Albanian)
Armenian
Balto-Slavic
Celtic
Germanic
Hellenic (Greek)
Romance
Indo-Iranian

Bulgarian
Czech
Latvian
Lithuanian
Polish
Russian
Serbo-Croatian
Slovenian
Slovak
Ukranian
Breton
Irish (Celtic)
Scottish (Celtic)
Welsh
Dutch
English
German
Scandinavian

Span./Port.
Romanian
French
Italian
Punjabi
Urdu
Pashto
Hindi
Bengali

Danish
Icelandic
Norwegian
Swedish

## ALPHABETS

An alphabet is a collection of letters or signs that stand for sounds in speech. Alphabets were developed from ancient picture-writing systems. The oldest letter is "O," unchanged in shape since it was used by the Phoenicians over 3,000 years ago.

▲ *Egyptian hieroglyphs or picture-signs are about 5,000 years old. The earliest signs represented objects.*

Russian

АБВГДЕЖЗИЙКЛМНОПРСТУФХЦЧ
ШЩЪЬЫЬЭЮЯ

Greek

ΑΒΓΔΕΖΗΘΙΚΛΜΝΞΟΠΡΣΤΥΦΧΨΩ

Arabic

ابتثجحخدذرزسشصضطظعغففقكلمنهو يلا

Bengali

আমাদের পোস্টমাস্টার কলিকাতার ছেলে । জলের
মাছকে ডাঙ্গায় তজলিলে যেরষ অবস্থা হয় এই গণ্ড
ধগরামের মধ্যে আসিয়া পোস্টমাস্টারেরও সেই দশা

## ARTIFICIAL LANGUAGES

Sign language is communication without speech. Finger-signing is a language used by deaf people.

"C" in both American and British sign language

"D" in British sign language

● There have been many attempts to invent artificial languages, such as Volapuk (1879) and Esperanto (1887). The inventors hoped a new language would help to break down old national rivalries.

● Esperanto has been the most successful artificial language, with some 10 million speakers. It has a 28-letter alphabet and its vocabulary contains many words common to the Indo-European group of languages. It was devised by a Pole, L.L. Zamenhof.

● Blind people can read and type using Braille, an alphabet of raised dots on paper invented by a young blind Frenchman, Louis Braille, in the 1820s. Blind people read Braille by running their fingertips over the dots. They can write Braille on a machine known as a Braillewriter.

## OTHER IMPORTANT LANGUAGES

**Afrikaans:** From 17th-century Dutch; spoken by many in South Africa.
**Gaelic:** Spoken in Ireland and Scotland.
**Greek:** Many English words derive from ancient Greek.
**Hebrew/Yiddish:** Hebrew is the language of the Bible and modern Israel.

**Latin:** Originally language of the ancient Romans.
**Sanskrit:** Language of ancient India, from *c.*1500 B.C.
**Pidgin:** Mixture of English and local words in the Pacific islands and New Guinea.
**Creole:** French, Spanish, and Portuguese mixed with local words in the Americas.

## THE WORLD'S MAJOR LANGUAGES

Mandarin, or standardized northern Chinese, is spoken by more people than any other language. English is the language spoken in the most countries (Australia, Canada, the Caribbean, Ireland, New Zealand, the U.K. and the U.S.A.). English is also widely used in parts of Africa and Asia. Hindi is the most widely spoken language of India. Spanish and Portuguese are spoken in Latin America, as well as in Spain and Portugal.

Millions of persons

Chinese 845 m.
English 485 m.
Hindi 338 m.
Spanish 331 m.
Russian 291 m.
Arabic 192 m.
Bengali 181 m.
Portuguese 171 m.
German 138 m.
Japanese 124 m.
French 118 m.
Malay-Indonesian 117 m.

900
800
700
600
500
400
300
200
100
0

# Religions

People in all times and cultures have tried to find the meaning of life. From this desire grew religious belief. Early religions were based on the worship of natural forces (the Sun, wind, and fire) and animals. Some religions have many gods; for example, modern Hinduism. Other faiths teach belief in one supreme god. Religion gives believers a moral code and the concept of a spiritual world beyond the earthly one. An atheist is a person who holds no religious belief; an agnostic is someone who is undecided.

## EARLY RELIGIONS

Early tribal religions, found worldwide, often involve beliefs in magic, witchcraft, and powerful spirits who may be good or evil and who dwell in animals, plants, rocks, and water.

Polynesian headdress worn in religious ceremonies

## MAJOR RELIGIONS

Christian Cross

Crescent Moon

Hindu god Siva

Statue of the Buddha

Taoist symbol of *yin* and *yang*

### CHRISTIANITY
Christianity is based on the life and teachings of Jesus Christ, born *c*.4 B.C. in Palestine and crucified by the Romans in *c*.A.D. 30. Christians believe that Jesus was the Son of God. Most Christians belong to one of three major groups: the Protestant, Roman Catholic, or Eastern Orthodox Churches.

### ISLAM
Founded in Arabia by the Prophet Muhammad in A.D. 622, the Islamic faith is derived largely from Judaism and Christianity. Islam's most sacred book is the Koran and its symbols are the crescent and the star. Followers of Islam are called Muslims, who submit to the will of God (Allah).

### HINDUISM
Hinduism is an ancient Indian religion with no known founder. It is the major religion in India and has had an important effect on Indian culture. Hindus worship many gods, most Hindus believing that all gods are aspects of Brahman, one universal spirit. They also believe in reincarnation of the soul after death.

### BUDDHISM
Buddhism is based on the teachings of an Indian, Siddhartha Gautama, in the 5th century B.C. The name Buddha means "Enlightened One." Buddhists do not believe in any god. Instead, they believe that people can attain enlightenment (nirvana) through meditation and the right actions.

### CHINESE
Taoism or Daoism is based on the teachings of Lao-tze who lived in China in the 6th century B.C. Believers yield to Tao, the "way" to restore harmony. The other Chinese ideology, Confucianism (from Confucius, also 500s B.C.), is a code of family and social behavior rather than a mystical faith.

### THE CITY OF MECCA
Islam has a number of holy cities, but none more sacred to Muslims than Mecca in Saudi Arabia, Muhammad's birthplace and the city from which he began his escape to Medina in A.D. 622. At least a million Muslims travel as pilgrims to Mecca every year; all Muslims are required to make a pilgrimage to Mecca once in their lifetime, if able to do so. The city's most sacred site is the Kaaba, a shrine that stands in the courtyard of the Great Mosque.

▲ *The Kaaba contains the Black Stone, by tradition given to Abraham by the angel Gabriel.*

### OTHER RELIGIONS
**Baha'i (Persian):** founded in the 1800s in what is now Iraq. The founder was a Persian, Bahaullah.
**Jainism (Indian):** a sect of Hinduism that teaches non-violence to all creatures.
**Shinto (Japanese):** Japan's oldest surviving religion. Shintoists worship their many gods (*kani*) at shrines or temples.

A Shinto pagoda (temple) in Japan

Membership of principal religions mid-1990

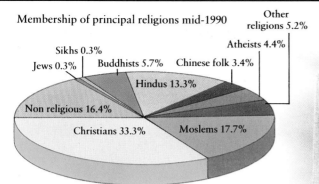

- Other religions 5.2%
- Atheists 4.4%
- Chinese folk 3.4%
- Sikhs 0.3%
- Jews 0.3%
- Buddhists 5.7%
- Hindus 13.3%
- Non religious 16.4%
- Christians 33.3%
- Moslems 17.7%

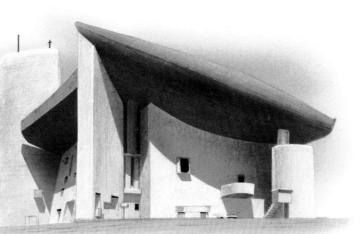

Star of David

Symbol of Sikhism

▲ *The pilgrimage chapel of Notre Dame du Haut is at Ronchamps in eastern France. The chapel is celebrated for its highly original style of church architecture; it was designed by France's most famous 20th-century architect, Le Corbusier, in the early 1950s.*

▼ *The Golden Temple in the sacred city of Amritsar in India is the holiest place of Sikh devotion. The city was built in the 1500s by the fourth Sikh guru (teacher), Ram Das. The temple stands on an island in a pool of fresh water, known as the "tank of immortality."*

## JUDAISM
The ancient religion of the Jews, founded by Moses and Abraham, was the first religion to teach that there is one God. The main laws of Judaism come from the Torah, the first five books of the Hebrew Bible (the Christian Old Testament). Jews worship in synagogues and in their homes; many Jews follow strict dietary laws.

## SIKHISM
A religion of India, the Sikhs' faith was first taught by Guru (teacher) Nanak (1469–1539). Nine gurus followed Nanak, but only God is considered the true guru. Sikhs have five "k" symbols: kesh (uncut hair), kangha (comb), kara (bracelet), kaccha (breeches), and kirpan (dagger).

## RELIGIONS: GLOSSARY
**Bible:** the holy book of both Christians and Jews.
**Caste:** religious and social division in Hinduism.
**Church:** place of Christian worship, or organized Christian group.
**Fast:** giving up food and drink as a part of religious observance.
**Hajj:** the Islamic pilgrimage to Mecca.
**Monks and nuns:** men and women, usually living in communities, who take religious vows.

**Mosque:** the place where Muslims worship.
**Pope:** head of the Roman Catholic Church.
**Orthodox Church:** the Eastern Christian Church that split from the Western Church in the 4th century; national Church of Russia, Greece, and Romania.
**Protestant:** a member of one of the Christian Churches that split from the Roman Catholic Church after the Reformation in the 1500s.

**Rabbi:** a Jewish religious leader or teacher.
**Saint:** a holy person worthy of worship.
**Vedas:** oldest and most sacred books of Hinduism.
**Zoroastrianism:** ancient religion of Iran founded by Zoroaster in the 500s B.C.

▶ *The Church of the Holy Family is in Barcelona in Spain. The architect, Antonio Gaudi, died in 1926 while construction was still in progress.*

# Customs and Celebrations

In all human societies, people mark the passage of time and the seasons by observing customs—such as having a feast to celebrate a good harvest. Our lives are marked by celebrations and festivals. We celebrate personal or family events, such as a birthday or a wedding. We observe national or religious holidays. Some of these customs are ancient. Their original meaning is forgotten as new beliefs and practices become more important. The variety of these celebrations adds color and significance to our lives.

### NON-RELIGIOUS FESTIVALS

Festivals usually take place once a year and last for at least a day. These include New Year, national holidays, independence days and legal holidays. Some festivals are connected to the history of a country, while others derive from seasonal feasts. Many festivals have moved far from their religious origins. For example, Halloween came from an early pagan festival, associated with the onset of winter and death. In the Middle Ages this became the Christian festival of All Saints' Day on November 1. The mass said on this day was *Allhallowmas* and the evening before became known as *Allhalloe'en*. In modern times, All Saints' Day is still a religious feast day, but in countries such as the United States Halloween is also a time when children put on costumes and play "trick or treat."

▲ *Once a Christian festival, Halloween (October 31) is now a time when children carve jack-o'-lanterns and attend Halloween parties.*

▼ *The eggs that are exchanged and eaten in many countries at Easter traditionally represent the renewal of life.*

▼ *The thrilling Palio horse race festival in Siena, Italy, has been held annually for hundreds of years.*

▲ *At carnival time in Rio de Janeiro, people in bright costumes fill the streets. Carnival, or Mardi Gras, marks the start of Lent.*

▼ *Every major religion has festivals or days of celebration. Some involve acts of pilgrimage by believers to holy places.*

### MAJOR RELIGIOUS FESTIVALS

#### CHRISTIANITY

**Christmas:** celebrates the birth of Christ. Customs such as Christmas trees and Santa Claus come from old midwinter festivals.
**Easter:** celebrates Christ's death and resurrection. More important than Christmas in the Orthodox Churches.

| ANIMAL | YEAR (The Chinese New Year starts in January or February) | | | | |
|---|---|---|---|---|---|
| Rat | 1936 | 1948 | 1960 | 1972 | 1984 |
| Ox | 1937 | 1949 | 1961 | 1973 | 1985 |
| Tiger | 1938 | 1950 | 1962 | 1974 | 1986 |
| Hare (Rabbit) | 1939 | 1951 | 1963 | 1975 | 1987 |
| Dragon | 1940 | 1952 | 1964 | 1976 | 1988 |
| Snake | 1941 | 1953 | 1965 | 1977 | 1989 |
| Horse | 1942 | 1954 | 1966 | 1978 | 1990 |
| Sheep (Goat) | 1943 | 1955 | 1967 | 1979 | 1991 |
| Monkey | 1944 | 1956 | 1968 | 1980 | 1992 |
| Rooster | 1945 | 1957 | 1969 | 1981 | 1993 |
| Dog | 1946 | 1958 | 1970 | 1982 | 1994 |
| Pig | 1947 | 1959 | 1971 | 1983 | 1995 |

**SOME FESTIVALS AND SPECIAL DAYS**

| | |
|---|---|
| **January:** | New Year's Day |
| | Martin Luther King Day (U.S.A.) |
| **February:** | St. Valentine's Day |
| **March:** | St. David's Day (Wales) |
| | St. Patrick's Day (Irl/U.S.A.) |
| **April:** | April Fool's Day |
| | St. George's Day (England) |
| **May:** | May Day, Mother's Day |
| **June:** | Father's Day (U.S.A./Can./U.K.) |
| **July:** | Independence Day (U.S.A.) |
| | Bastille Day (France) |
| **September:** | Labor Day (U.S.A.) |
| **October:** | Oktoberfest (Germany), |
| | Halloween |
| **November:** | Armistice/Veterans' Day |
| | Thanksgiving Day (U.S.A.) |
| | St. Andrew's Day (Scotland) |
| **December:** | Boxing Day (U.K./Canada) |
| | New Year's Eve |
| | (Hogmanay in Scotland) |

▲ *The Chinese calendar is based on the lunar year. It begins at 2637 B.C. (traditionally, the year of its invention by the first emperor). The years run in cycles of 60, and involve the names of 12 animals.*

▶ *On Independence Day, July 4th, Americans enjoy parades, picnics, pageants, and fireworks.*

| BUDDHISM | JUDAISM | HINDUISM | ISLAM |
|---|---|---|---|
|  |  |  |  |

**BUDDHISM**

**Wesak or Vesakha-puja:** (Sri Lanka and Thailand) celebrates the birth, enlightenment and death of Buddha.
**Flower festival:** (Japan) celebrates Buddha's birth.
**Rites of passage:** (Japan) a child's coming of age.

**JUDAISM**

**Rosh Hashanah:** Jewish New Year.
**Passover:** commemorates the Exodus from Egypt.
**Hanukkah and Purim:** God's deliverance of the Jews in 165 B.C.
**Yom Kippur:** a day of regret for faults.

**HINDUISM**

**Navarati:** in honor of goddess Shakti.
**Dusserah:** honoring Prince Rama.
**Holi:** an exuberant spring festival.
**Diwali:** festival of lights. There are many regional festivals.

**ISLAM**

**The Great Festival:** a time of sacrifice and giving to the poor after pilgrimage to the city of Mecca (which all Muslims try to make).
**The Lesser Festival:** Breaking of the Fast— marking the end of the fasting month of Ramadan.

# Arts and Crafts

The visual arts, painting and sculpture, are ancient arts: there are carvings and cave paintings over 15,000 years old. Pottery and architecture developed when people first became settled farmers, about 10,000 years ago. The performing arts include music, dance, theater, and motion pictures. The first three all have their origins in our prehistoric past; motion pictures (and radio and television) are 20th-century inventions. Literature began with storytelling; writing was only invented 5,000 years ago.

## VISUAL ARTS

The visual arts include painting, sculpture, ceramics, and textiles. Traditional arts (carpets or masks, for example) may change little in style over the centuries. Painters and sculptors have constantly sought fresh ways to express their vision of the world.

▲ *An American porcelain plate. Fine porcelain is also made in Europe and Asia.*

◄ *A ceremonial mask made by the BaLuba of Central Africa.*

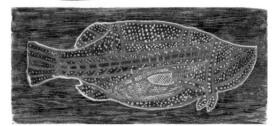

◄ *Venetians have been known for making beautiful glass since the 1200s.*

▲ *This selection of crafts from around the world includes a rug made by the Navajo people of New Mexico and Arizona (above); a neck ornament in gold and silver from Kashmir in Asia (right); and a bark painting made by an Aboriginal artist in Australia (left).*

## THE PERFORMING ARTS

Dance was originally part of tribal ritual. It developed into drama—literature acted out with words and often accompanied by music. Western drama began in ancient Greece some 2,500 years ago. Eastern drama includes the Kabuki and Noh theater of Japan. The earliest written music is Indian, 3,000 years old. Ballet and opera developed in Europe during the 1400s and 1500s.

◄ *Kabuki actors in Japan, where these colorful melodramas have been performed since the 1600s.*

▶ *A musician plays an important instrument in Indian music, the sitar, or Indian lute.*

## FACTS ABOUT THE ARTS

- English speakers wrote in Latin before the 1300s. Geoffrey Chaucer's *Canterbury Tales* (*c.*1387), written in English, was a landmark in the use of everyday language.
- About 800,000 people heard an open-air concert by the New York Philharmonic Orchestra in Central Park, New York, in 1986. This is thought to be the largest ever audience for a classical concert.
- Before graphite pencils became available in the 1600s, artists sketched with a metal silverpoint on prepared paper.
- The oldest piano in the world is one made by the Italian Bartolommeo Cristofori in 1720; it is now in New York's Metropolitan Museum.
- The largest library in the world is the United States Library of Congress, with 97.5 million items.
- Walt Disney (1906–1966), the cartoon and movie producer, won a record 32 Oscar awards.
- Wood-carving is probably the best known form of African sculpture. But artists in the Benin kingdom in West Africa (1500–1700) produced superb metalwork.
- The first purpose-built movie theater was opened at the Atlanta Show in Georgia in 1895.
- The most successful rock group to date are the Beatles (John Lennon, Paul McCartney, Ringo Starr, and George Harrison) with sales of over a billion tapes and discs as a group, and millions more as solo performers.

▶ *Watched by an audience of about 200,000 in Berlin, Germany, Pink Floyd's performance of "The Wall" in 1990 was the biggest ever rock concert, involving 600 performers.*

## LITERATURE

The first writings were practical records and business documents. Creative writing came later, in the form of songs and stories recording epic deeds, great kings, and ancient folk-memories. Poetry (easier to recite and remember) came before prose. All major languages of East and West have literatures, each with their own major dramatists, novelists, and poets. Critics generally agree that the English dramatist William Shakespeare (1564–1616) is the world's greatest playwright. As well as plays such as *Romeo and Juliet, Hamlet, Macbeth,* and *A Midsummer's Night Dream*, he is also known for his poetry, such as the *Sonnets* (1609).

## ARTS FESTIVALS

In the past, artists such as musicians and painters were often supported by wealthy patrons. Today, few artists can expect such backing. Arts festivals provide venues for artists to come together to exhibit and perform. Some festivals specialize: the Newport Jazz Festival in Rhode Island, for example, or the Salzburg Music Festival in Austria, which celebrates the music of Mozart. Others, such as Scotland's Edinburgh Festival, are showplaces for artists and performers from the theater, musical arts, visual arts, comedy and literature.

▶ *The annual Edinburgh Festival Fringe—which includes music, art, drama, and comedy—is the world's biggest arts festival.*

| | |
|---|---|
| **All Arts:** | Edinburgh (Scotland) |
| | Avignon (France) |
| | Osaka (Japan) |
| **Film:** | Cannes (France) |
| | Berlin (Germany) |
| | Venice (Italy) |
| **Music:** | Salzburg [Mozart] (Austria) |
| | Bayreuth [Wagner] (Germany) |
| | Aldeburgh [classical] (England) |
| | Tanglewood [classical] (U.S.A.) |
| | Newport R.I. [jazz] (U.S.A.) |
| | Aix-en-Provence [classical] (France) |
| **Television:** | Montreux (Switzerland) |
| **Theater:** | Stratford [Shakespeare] (Ont., Canada) |

# RESOURCES

## Farming

The Earth is rich in resources such as farmland, minerals, and energy. Yet the world population is growing so fast and consuming these resources so quickly that we must learn to conserve them. Farmers produce most of our food, and many of the materials in the products we use. Important food crops grown worldwide include cereals (wheat, corn, and rice), root crops (potatoes and sassava), pulses (beans and peas), fruits and vegetables, oil crops such as soybeans, sugar from cane and beet, nuts, and crops such as tea and coffee.

Livestock includes cattle, chickens, pigs, sheep, and goats. Fertile farmland and food resources are unevenly spread around the world. Europe, North America, and Australasia produce more than enough to feed their people. But in poorer countries farmers may lack resources and often cannot even feed their own families.

| LEADING PRODUCERS | Wheat 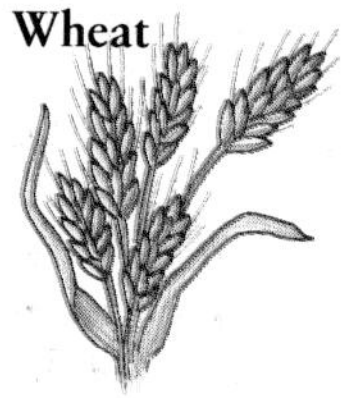 | Rice  | Potatoes  | Sugar 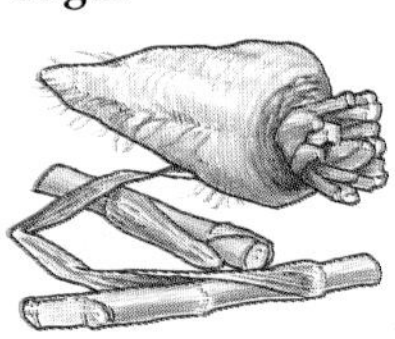 | Soybeans  | Wine  |
|---|---|---|---|---|---|---|
| 1st | C.I.S. | China | C.I.S. | Brazil | U.S.A. | Italy |
| 2nd | China | India | Poland | India | Brazil | France |
| 3rd | U.S.A. | Indonesia | China | C.I.S. | China | Spain |

**WORLD CROP OUTPUT**

Asia 43%
Europe and C.I.S. 27%
Africa 7%
Australia and Oceania 2%
South and Central America 10%
U.S.A. and Canada 11%

▲ *The top three producers of six agricultural products: wheat, rice, potatoes, sugar, soybeans and wine. (C.I.S. = Commonwealth of Independent States, formerly the U.S.S.R.).*

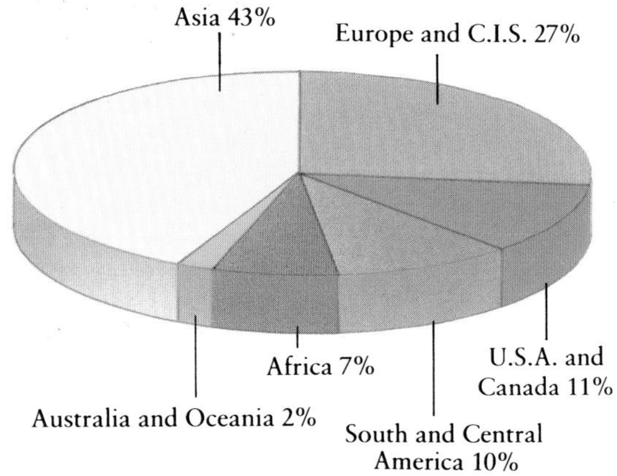

▶ *Terraced rice fields allow the maximum use of hillside farmland.*

▶ *People are eating more poultry, but less beef and pork. The U.S.A., C.I.S., China, Brazil and France have 60 percent of the world's chickens. Europe leads in the production of dairy foods (butter, milk, and cheese). India has most cattle but India's Hindus do not eat beef.*

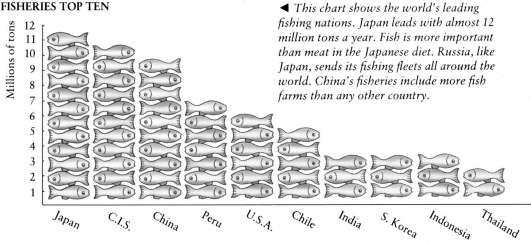

| LEADING PRODUCERS | Cattle | Pigs | Sheep | Poultry | Goats |
|---|---|---|---|---|---|
| 1st | U.S.A. | China | Australia | U.S.A. | India |
| 2nd | C.I.S. | C.I.S. | C.I.S. | C.I.S. | China |
| 3rd | Brazil | U.S.A. | China | Brazil | Pakistan |

## FISHERIES TOP TEN

Millions of tons

12 11 10 9 8 7 6 5 4 3 2 1

Japan, C.I.S., China, Peru, U.S.A., Chile, India, S. Korea, Indonesia, Thailand

◀ *This chart shows the world's leading fishing nations. Japan leads with almost 12 million tons a year. Fish is more important than meat in the Japanese diet. Russia, like Japan, sends its fishing fleets all around the world. China's fisheries include more fish farms than any other country.*

### FOOD AID
Many people in poorer countries eat less than 2,000 calories a day. The daily requirement for a healthy diet is 3,000 for a man and 2,200 for a woman. Food aid from wealthier countries helps some of the world's hungry to survive.

## HOW MANY PEOPLE WORK ON THE LAND?

Percentage of population employed in farming (1990)

Developed countries 8.4%

Developing countries 59.6%

◀ *In the poorer countries, roughly half the population works on the land. Many are subsistence farmers, growing only enough food to support their own families. In the richer parts of the world (North America, Europe, and Australia), farms are usually larger and are run as businesses. Machines do most of the work, so they need few workers.*

◀ *Portuguese fishermen sort their catch. Over-fishing has reduced fish stocks in many seas. Fish must be conserved, not hunted to extinction. One solution is more fish farming.*

▼ *Combines harvest wheat in North America. World wheat production is around 600 million tons a year. China grows the most wheat, but North America is the biggest exporter.*

# Materials and Minerals

Timber is a precious material which can be renewed. Metals and minerals cannot be replaced once they have been mined: they include iron ore, copper, tin, gold, building stone, and phosphates. Mining methods include deep-pit, open-pit, strip (surface) mining, dredging, and quarrying. Two key materials are petroleum and bauxite. Petroleum is burned as a fuel; its by-products include many chemicals and plastics. From bauxite ore comes aluminum, a metal used to make many different goods.

### FACTS ABOUT MINING

- The leading mining state for petroleum and gas in the United States is Texas.
- South Africa mines the world's most gold.
- The deepest coal shaft (7,000 ft./2,042 m) is in the Donbas coalfield in the Ukraine.
- Australia produces the most diamonds and bauxite of any country in the world.
- Canada mines the most uranium and zinc.

▶ *Most exported tropical hardwoods go to Japan; most of the rest go to China and Europe. Countries such as Brazil, the Philippines, and Malaysia provide 70 percent of tropical hardwood exports. By 2000 the Philippines may have no usable forests left.*

▶ *In the developing world many people burn wood for fuel. Over 90 percent of India's timber-cut is burned for cooking.*

▼ *Rain forests are being felled at an alarming rate. The Amazon forest is the world's biggest natural plant resource.*

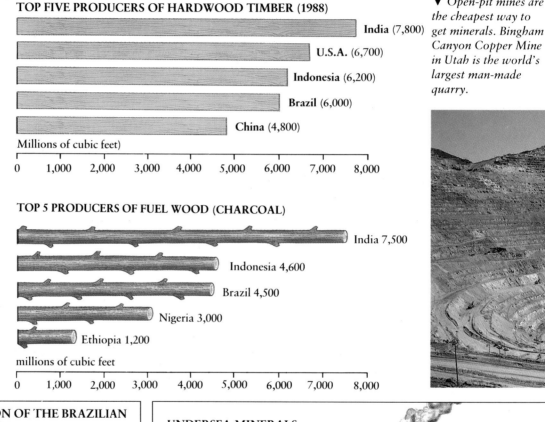

**TOP FIVE PRODUCERS OF HARDWOOD TIMBER (1988)**

India (7,800)
U.S.A. (6,700)
Indonesia (6,200)
Brazil (6,000)
China (4,800)

Millions of cubic feet)

0   1,000   2,000   3,000   4,000   5,000   6,000   7,000   8,000

**TOP 5 PRODUCERS OF FUEL WOOD (CHARCOAL)**

India 7,500
Indonesia 4,600
Brazil 4,500
Nigeria 3,000
Ethiopia 1,200

millions of cubic feet

0   1,000   2,000   3,000   4,000   5,000   6,000   7,000   8,000

▼ *Open-pit mines are the cheapest way to get minerals. Bingham Canyon Copper Mine in Utah is the world's largest man-made quarry.*

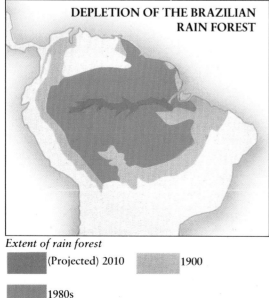

## DEPLETION OF THE BRAZILIAN RAIN FOREST

Extent of rain forest

(Projected) 2010    1900

1980s

## UNDERSEA MINERALS

Mineral resources on land are being used up at an alarming rate. For new sources, future generations may turn to the oceans. The valuable minerals found on land can also be extracted from the sea (although this is costly). About 20 percent of the world's oil comes from undersea wells. Huge reserves of minerals also lie deep on the seabed in the form of manganese nodules.

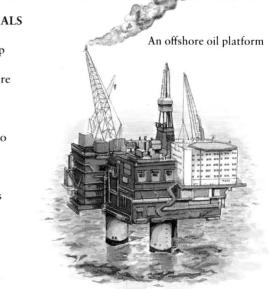

An offshore oil platform

## MAJOR OIL PRODUCERS

The leading producers of crude (unrefined) oil are the U.S.A. and Saudi Arabia. Together the C.I.S. republics produce more.

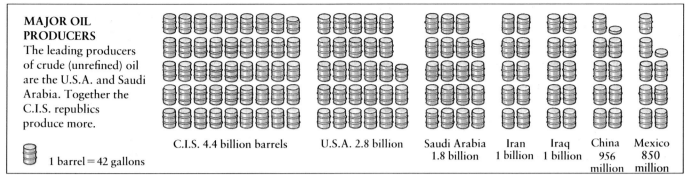

1 barrel = 42 gallons

C.I.S. 4.4 billion barrels | U.S.A. 2.8 billion | Saudi Arabia 1.8 billion | Iran 1 billion | Iraq 1 billion | China 956 million | Mexico 850 million

▶ *There are about 3,000 different kinds of minerals. About a hundred minerals are quite common and those such as aluminum and iron are used in enormous amounts. Other minerals (such as titanium) are relatively scarce. The chart lists important minerals, their uses, and the world's leading producers.*

## COAL PRODUCTION

The U.S.A. and Australia are the world's leading exporters of coal. Canada, Poland, South Africa, Russia, and Ukraine are also big exporters. China digs and burns more coal than any other nation. Coal production worldwide has risen since the 1970s, but the price of coal is being increased by environmental costs, such as clean-air scrubbers in coal-burning power stations. Also, as surface deposits are used up, mines are being dug more deeply, even though deep-pit mining costs more than open-pit or strip mining.

## LEADING COAL PRODUCERS (million tons)

China 956 | U.S.A. 862 | C.I.S. (mostly Russia and Ukraine) 785 | Germany 500 | Poland 284

| METALS | USES | LEADING PRODUCERS |
|---|---|---|
| Aluminum | power cables, cooking foil, tennis rackets, food packaging, cans | U.S.A., C.I.S., Canada, Australia, Brazil |
| Chromium | plating on metals, as an alloy to make stainless steel, as leather tanning | South Africa, Zimbabwe |
| Copper | electrical wiring, machinery, in alloys (bronze, brass), insecticides, paint | Chile, U.S.A., Canada, C.I.S., Zambia, Zaire |
| Gold | currency, jewelry, gold leaf (alloyed with copper or silver), electronics | South Africa, C.I.S., Canada, U.S.A., China, Australia |
| Iron | cast iron (molded), wrought iron. Most iron used in steel-making | C.I.S., Brazil, Australia China, Canada South Africa, Sweden |
| Lead | lead acid batteries, gasoline additive (declining), paints, machine bearings | U.S.A., C.I.S., Australia Canada, Peru, China, Mexico, North Korea |
| Manganese | compounds of manganese in dry batteries, paints; vital alloy in steel-making | C.I.S., South Africa Brazil, India China, Australia |
| Nickel | electroplating (stainless), dry batteries, as an alloy in steel-making | C.I.S., Canada, Australia New Caledonia |
| Platinum | chemical containers, jewelry, surgical instruments, electronics | C.I.S., South Africa, Canada, Japan, Australia |
| Silver | in coinage, jewelry, dentistry, photo film, batteries, electronics | Mexico, Peru, C.I.S., U.S.A., Canada, Poland, Australia |
| Tin | on steel cans, in solder (with lead), in bronze, toothpaste, roofing | Malaysia, Peru, C.I.S., Indonesia, Brazil, China, Australia |
| Titanium | titanium dioxide in paint, paint, paper, tools, as an alloy in aircraft | C.I.S., Japan, U.S.A., U.K., China |
| Zinc | in alloys (brass, with copper), batteries, paints, electroplating, cosmetics | Canada, C.I.S., Australia, Peru, China Mexico, Chile |

# Energy

The world relies heavily for energy on "fossil fuels," such as coal, natural gas, and petroleum. These fuels were formed millions of years ago. Existing reserves may be exhausted in between 100 and 300 years. Untapped reserves would be very expensive to extract. We therefore need to use alternative energy sources (solar, wave, and wind power) in order to conserve fossil fuel reserves. Nuclear power once promised cheap, limitless energy, but its future now looks uncertain because of costs and concerns about its safety.

### FACTS ABOUT ENERGY

● Energy is measured in units called joules (J) named after the British scientist James Prescott Joule (1818–1889).
● The watt (W) is a unit of power—the rate of producing or using energy—and is commonly used for measuring electric power. The watt is named after steam pioneer James Watt (1736–1819).

## WORLD ENERGY CONSUMPTION

Energy in gigajoules

200 or more
100–200
50–100
15–50
Less than 15
Figures not available

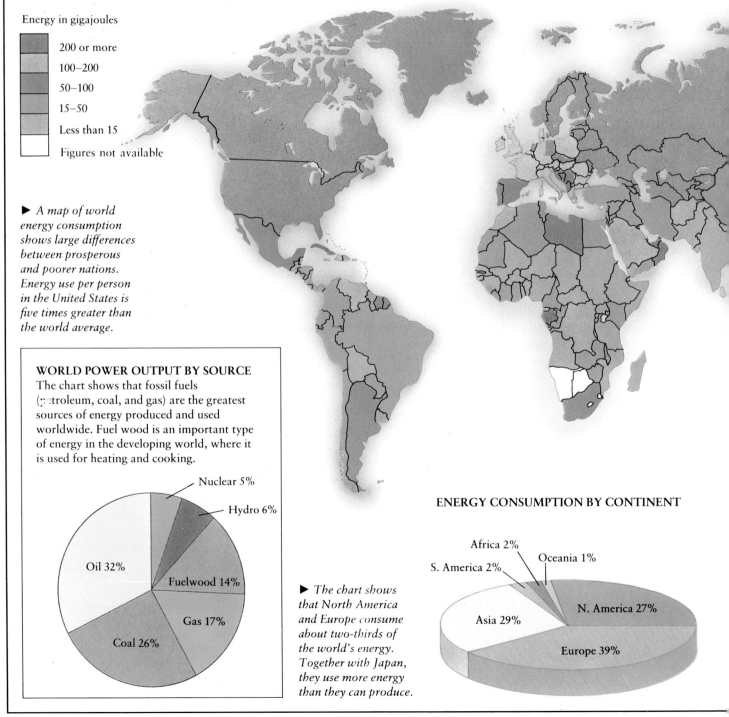

▶ *A map of world energy consumption shows large differences between prosperous and poorer nations. Energy use per person in the United States is five times greater than the world average.*

### WORLD POWER OUTPUT BY SOURCE
The chart shows that fossil fuels (petroleum, coal, and gas) are the greatest sources of energy produced and used worldwide. Fuel wood is an important type of energy in the developing world, where it is used for heating and cooking.

Nuclear 5%
Hydro 6%
Oil 32%
Fuelwood 14%
Gas 17%
Coal 26%

▶ *The chart shows that North America and Europe consume about two-thirds of the world's energy. Together with Japan, they use more energy than they can produce.*

### ENERGY CONSUMPTION BY CONTINENT

Africa 2%
Oceania 1%
S. America 2%
Asia 29%
N. America 27%
Europe 39%

## NUCLEAR ENERGY

In a commercial nuclear reactor, the energy produced by the fission (splitting) of uranium atoms heats water to make steam to drive electricity generators. The first reactor was built at the University of Chicago in 1942. In recent years, rising costs and safety fears have made nuclear energy less attractive, although nuclear fusion (the joining together of atomic nuclei) may be an option for the next century.

**TOP 6 NUCLEAR POWER PRODUCERS** (amount per year in kilowatt-hours (kw/h))

|  | |  |
|---|---|---|
| U.S.A. | ☢☢☢☢☢☢☢☢☢☢☢☢☢ | 527 billion |
| France | ☢☢☢☢☢☢ | 260 billion |
| C.I.S. | ☢☢☢☢☢ | 204 billion |
| Japan | ☢☢☢☢ | 164 billion |
| Germany | ☢☢☢ | 137 billion |
| Canada | ☢☢ | 78 billion |

☢ = 40 billion kw/h

◄ *Nuclear plants produce radioactivity and deadly waste. An accident, such as that at Chernobyl in Russia (1986) has disastrous consequences.*

◄ *The 12,600,000-kilowatt Itaipu Dam power plant on the Parana River in Brazil is the world's most powerful hydroelectric dam. A hydroelectric dam can provide water as well as electricity.*

## HYDROELECTRIC POWER

Most hydroelectric schemes involve the construction of huge dams to store water in artificial lakes. The water is released under great pressure to drive turbines that generate electricity. Some countries, Brazil for example, generate as much as 80 percent of their energy from water power.

1 megawatt (M.W) = 1 million watts

| DAM | COUNTRY | OUTPUT |
|---|---|---|
| Guri Dam | Venezuela | 10,300 MW |
| Grand Coulee | U.S.A. | 7460 MW* |
| Itaipu | Brazil/Paraguay | 7400 MW** |
| Sayano-Shushensk | Russia | 6400 MW |
| Krasnoyarsk | Russia | 6000 MW |

\* upgrading to 12,600 MW   \*\*upgrading to 10,800 MW

## ALTERNATIVE POWER

On a wind farm a windmill called a wind turbine produces power as its blades turn in the wind. Our search for "greener" energy sources (such as wind, tide, and solar power) is spurred by the knowledge that oil and coal will not last for ever. Wind power is practical in some areas: one generator can light 2,000 homes.

◄ *Turbines on a wind farm on Long Island. Most wind turbines have two propeller-shaped blades.*

# Trade and Industry

The nations of the world live by trading goods such as cars and cotton, and by supplying services such as insurance and vacations. Goods and services are products of industry. Manufacturing—making things—is important to most industrial economies, and depends on supplies of raw materials, such as oil and coal. Some countries have a lot of raw materials, while others have almost none. Countries such as Japan and Singapore can still prosper from trade despite having few natural resources of their own.

**MAJOR INDUSTRIAL AREAS**

■ Major industrial areas

**MAJOR INDUSTRIAL AREAS**

**North America:** The United States is the most powerful industrial nation. Its main manufacturing regions are in the north-east, midwest, and on the west coast. Manufacturing employs a total of 17 percent of U.S. workers.

**South America:** Brazil is the continent's major manufacturer, followed by Argentina.

**Europe:** Europe, particularly in the west, has a powerful industrial economy. The EC dominates trade and industry; Germany is Europe's industrial leader.

**Asia:** Japan is the most successful trading nation. It is the world's biggest producer of vehicles, ships, and TV sets. Singapore, South Korea, and Taiwan all have thriving manufacturing export industries. China still relies mainly on state-run factories.

**Russia:** The industrial giant of the former U.S.S.R. It has high technology in some areas (space technology), but needs to modernize its financial structure and its industries.

**Pacific:** Australia, Indonesia, and Philippines are the main industrial countries.

**Africa:** Some African states have very little industry. The North African countries have oil-based economies. Egypt and Nigeria are industrial, but South Africa is by far the richest manufacturing country.

## MAJOR SECTORS IN TRADE AND INDUSTRY

**Advertising:** Goods have been advertised since pre-Roman times when people first hung signs outside their shops. The largest neon sign in the world today is an advertisement for cigarettes in Hong Kong.

**Aerospace:** The world's biggest aircraft producer is Boeing.

**Banks:** The bank with the most branches is the State Bank of India (over 12,400 branches).

**Cars:** The General Motors Corporation of Detroit is the biggest industrial company of the world. Apart from vehicles, General Motors is involved in defense equipment, computer services and aircraft, and has more than 750,000 employees.

**Clothing:** The biggest U.S. clothing manufacturer is Levi Strauss, best known for its jeans.

**Games and toys:** This industry is dominated by Asian factories making toys for Western markets.

**Petrochemicals:** Oil-rich nations such as Saudi Arabia are diversifying into petrochemicals.

**Medicinal drugs:** The world's largest pharmaceutical company is Johnson & Johnson (U.S.A.).

**Removals:** The Shore Porters' Society of Aberdeen, Scotland, has been carrying and storing people's goods since before 1498.

**Retail:** The largest retail company in the world is Sears, Roebuck, and Co., of Chicago. The company was founded in 1886 and is noted for its mail order catalog business as well as its stores.

**Shipbuilding:** Japan builds roughly 40 percent of the world's new ships.

**Steel:** The biggest producer is Japan's Nippon Steel Corporation.

**Telecommunications:** Japan makes the most TV sets, producing nearly 18 million a year.

**Tourism:** Americans earn more than any other country from tourism and spend most on it, too.

▲ *About $110 billion is spent on advertising in the United States each year. These giant neon advertisements are in New York's Times Square.*

## MAJOR EXPORTING COUNTRIES

■ Major exporters of primary (raw) materials

■ Major exporters of manufactured goods

▲ *This map illustrates how raw materials and manufactured goods move between developed and developing nations. In general, developing countries supply raw materials, not finished goods. Japan, the world's most successful trader, relies heavily on imported raw materials.*

▶ *In poor and rich nations alike, roads carry most goods. Farms and factories use trucks to transport their products.*

▼ *Cargo ships carry bulky freight. Ships using the Panama Canal can take a short route between the Pacific and the Atlantic oceans.*

### FACTS ABOUT TRADE AND INDUSTRY

- The world's largest employer is Indian Railways, with 1.6 million people.
- Although agriculture is often called the oldest industry, the earliest evidence of farming is in about 9000 B.C., thousands of years after people began to produce stone tools.
- With an output of over 8 million cars a year, Japan makes more cars than any other country.
- The developing world has only about 14 percent of the world's industry. Many poor countries produce only one main export item: for example, 62 different countries compete to sell coffee abroad.
- The Faversham Oyster Company in England claims to have existed from "time immemorial." In English law this means before 1189, making the firm the world's oldest company.

# Money and Debt

The world is growing richer. There are 20 times more goods and services today than there were in 1900. The few rich countries dominate the world economy. Poor countries borrow to finance development and are often unable to pay increasing debts. National wealth is compared by looking at gross national product (GNP) per head of population. For example, Switzerland (over $35,000 worth of output per person per year) is much richer than Ethiopia (about $120 per person per year).

## POPULAR CURRENCIES

Many countries use the same name for their money. The United States, Australia, Fiji, Jamaica, Singapore, and Zimbabwe have dollars. France, Belgium, and several African countries use francs. Dinars are used in Algeria, Iraq, Jordan, and Tunisia. Ireland, Lebanon and Syria, as well as the U.K., have pounds. Other currencies, such as Poland's zloty or Japan's yen, are unique.

## AVERAGE WEALTH PER PERSON PER COUNTRY (PER CAPITA GNP)

### WHAT IS GNP?

Gross national product (GNP) is what a country earns in a year. Divide by population to find the per capita (per head) figure. The map (right) shows how wealth is spread. Europe, North America, Japan, and Australia have the highest per person GNPs in the world.

U.S.$, 1988

| | |
|---|---|
| 20,000 and over | 1500–2999 |
| 10,000–19,999 | 500–1499 |
| 5000–9999 | Under 500 |
| 3000–4999 | Figures not available |

## THE EARLIEST MONEY

- The first trade was done without money, by barter (exchange). Coins were first used in ancient Greece, India, and China, where people used metal shaped like tools as money as early as 1100 B.C.
- The Chinese invented paper money in the A.D. 800s. The Chinese use of paper money instead of coins amazed the Italian traveler Marco Polo in the 1200s. Europeans did not use paper money until the 1600s, when the first bank notes were issued.

## THE RICH GET RICHER

Taking the world as a whole, average income per person has doubled since 1950. But while an American is three times richer today than in 1950, an Ethiopian is no better off.

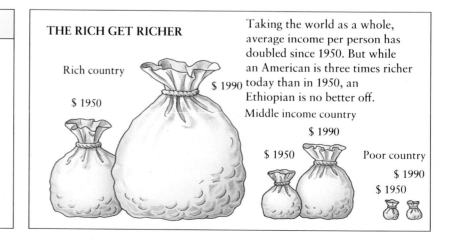

Rich country
$ 1950
$ 1990

Middle income country
$ 1990
$ 1950

Poor country
$ 1990
$ 1950

## AID AND DEBT

Many poorer nations are deep in debt, owing far more than they originally borrowed. As oil prices rose in the 1970s, developing nations borrowed to meet higher oil bills, and to finance development projects such as dams. When interest rates rose and world trade slumped, these countries faced crippling debt burdens. Aid can be measured in total cash given, or as a percentage of national income. The United States, Japan, France, and Germany give the most aid; Norway comes top in terms of percentage of GNP (1.17 percent).

▼ On the trading floor of the Paris Bourse in France, vast amounts of money change hands every hour on the world's money and stock markets.

## LEADING CONTRIBUTORS TO OVERSEAS AID (1988)

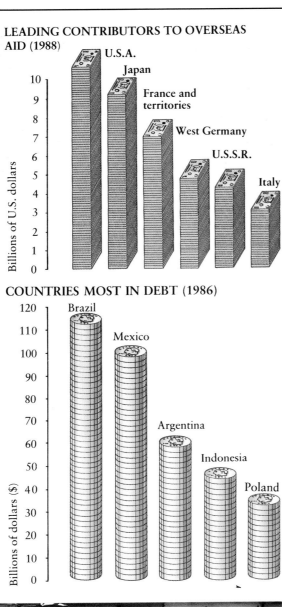

Billions of U.S. dollars

U.S.A.
Japan
France and territories
West Germany
U.S.S.R.
Italy

## COUNTRIES MOST IN DEBT (1986)

Billions of dollars ($)

Brazil
Mexico
Argentina
Indonesia
Poland

### FACTS ABOUT MONEY

- The Group of Seven or G7 nations (the richest) are the U.S.A., Japan, Germany, France, Britain, Canada, and Italy.
- The gulf between the richest and poorest can be huge. In Brazil the richest 20 percent of the population earn 28 times more than the poorest 20 percent.
- Nearly 50 countries, mainly in Africa and Asia, have per capita GNPs of below $500.
- The world's richest country in terms of per capita GNP is Switzerland: $35,000. The poorest is Mozambique, where per capita GNP is only $80.
- The biggest bank in the world is the World Bank, or the International Bank of Reconstruction and Development, founded in 1945. An agency of the UN, the bank lends money to countries for essential projects such as irrigation schemes.

▲ Although every country has its own system of money, all use coins and paper money that have little value on their own.

- The term "millionaire" was first used in the mid 1700s. The very rich are often rather secretive about their wealth, but among the world's richest people are Yoshiaki Tsutsumi of Japan and the Sultan of Brunei, each of whom boasts a fortune of over $16 billion. The richest woman in the world is said to be Britain's Queen Elizabeth, though only a proportion of her assets (worth $10 billion) are personal.
- The country with the largest gold reserves is the United States, with about a quarter of the world's gold. These reserves are stored in standard bars of 27.43 pounds at the U.S. Army base at Fort Knox in Kentucky. Fort Knox, understandably, ranks among the most secure buildings in the world.

# Education and Health

A rich nation should have educated and healthy citizens. A poor nation also aspires to such ideals, but faces daunting problems. Poor countries have too few doctors and hospitals, too few teachers and schools. Every year nearly 5 million children in the developing world die from diarrhea, caused in most cases by drinking unclean water. Education is particularly important—without it, hopes of a better life cannot be fulfilled. More than a quarter of the world's people cannot read and write.

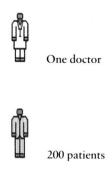

One doctor

200 patients

▼ *The illustration below compares the number of patients to doctors in selected countries. Burkina Faso, a poor country in West Africa, is typical of many African states: it has only one doctor for every 30,000 people. Compare the ratio of doctors to patients in the U.S. or Germany.*

## PEOPLE PER DOCTOR (SELECTED COUNTRIES)

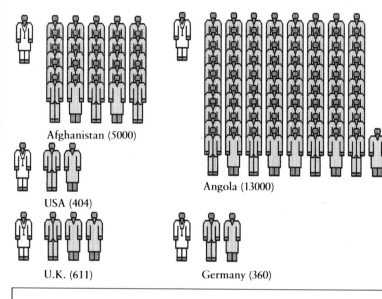

Afghanistan (5000)

USA (404)

U.K. (611)

Angola (13000)

Germany (360)

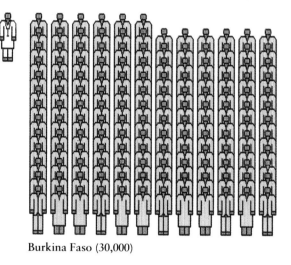

Burkina Faso (30,000)

## HOSPITAL BEDS

A hospital cannot function without trained doctors and nurses, medicines and clean water, laundry, and power. In parts of the developing world a sick person has little hope of a hospital bed. In Afghanistan there are five beds for every 10,000 people. In Norway 152 beds serve the same number of people.

▼ *A ward in a British eye hospital. Even if they have to go onto a waiting list, people in richer countries eventually get a hospital bed.*

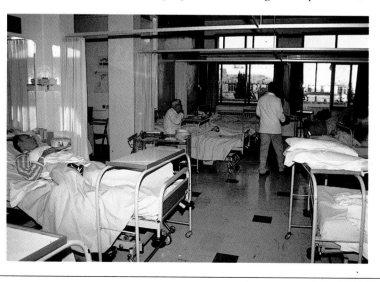

## HEALTH AND WELFARE

Rich countries can afford to fund health and welfare programs for their citizens—providing pensions for the elderly and payments to mothers of young children, for example. The table below contrasts what Australia and Ethiopia can afford as benefits to their people.

| BENEFIT | Australia | Ethiopia |
|---|---|---|
| Work injury | ✓ | ✓ |
| Old age pension | ✓ | ✗ |
| Sickness/maternity benefit | ✓ | ✗ |
| Unemployment benefit | ✓ | ✗ |
| Family allowance | ✓ | ✗ |

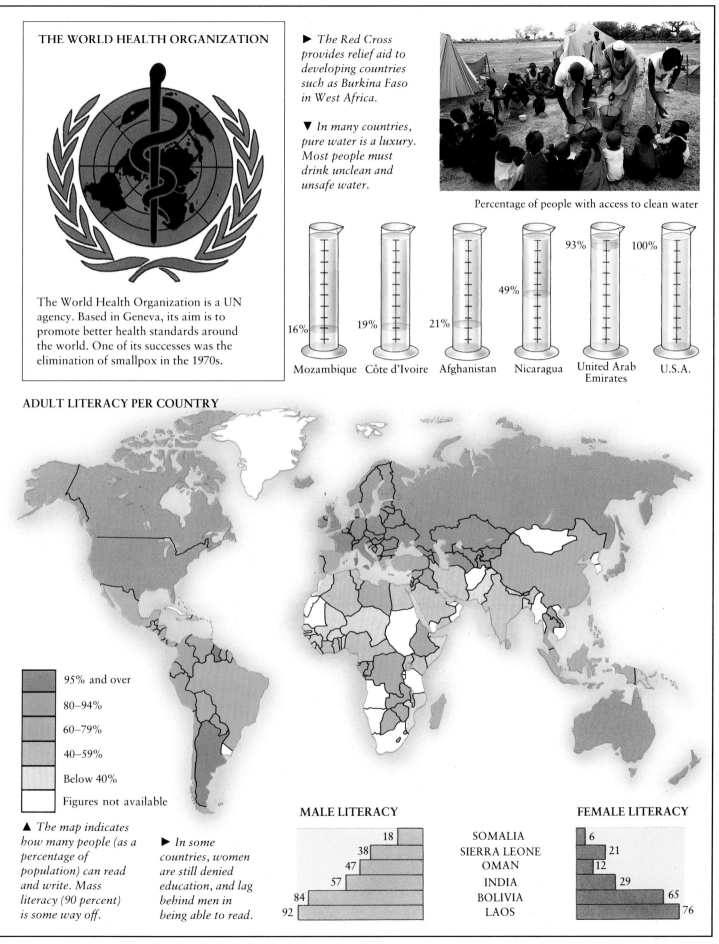

## THE WORLD HEALTH ORGANIZATION

The World Health Organization is a UN agency. Based in Geneva, its aim is to promote better health standards around the world. One of its successes was the elimination of smallpox in the 1970s.

► *The Red Cross provides relief aid to developing countries such as Burkina Faso in West Africa.*

▼ *In many countries, pure water is a luxury. Most people must drink unclean and unsafe water.*

Percentage of people with access to clean water

| Mozambique | Côte d'Ivoire | Afghanistan | Nicaragua | United Arab Emirates | U.S.A. |
|---|---|---|---|---|---|
| 16% | 19% | 21% | 49% | 93% | 100% |

## ADULT LITERACY PER COUNTRY

95% and over
80–94%
60–79%
40–59%
Below 40%
Figures not available

▲ *The map indicates how many people (as a percentage of population) can read and write. Mass literacy (90 percent) is some way off.*

► *In some countries, women are still denied education, and lag behind men in being able to read.*

### MALE LITERACY

| | |
|---|---|
| 18 | SOMALIA |
| 38 | SIERRA LEONE |
| 47 | OMAN |
| 57 | INDIA |
| 84 | BOLIVIA |
| 92 | LAOS |

### FEMALE LITERACY

| | |
|---|---|
| SOMALIA | 6 |
| SIERRA LEONE | 21 |
| OMAN | 12 |
| INDIA | 29 |
| BOLIVIA | 65 |
| LAOS | 76 |

73

# POLITICS

## Government

Governments exist because society needs a structure to make laws, defend its citizens, set taxes, and spend money for the common good. Early governments were authoritarian, imposed by powerful rulers. The ancient Greeks were the first civilization to experiment with democracy, or rule by the people, and today democracy still survives in various forms. The most common form of government worldwide is the republic, with an elected lawmaking government and president. Central to the idea of democracy is the concept of choice: political ideas are put forward by parties and chosen or rejected by voters in elections. Most true democracies have two or more political parties. However, one-party states are plentiful and, despite losing its grip in Europe, Communism still has a stronghold in the world's most populous country, China.

### TYPES OF GOVERNMENT

- Monarchy
- Federal constitutional monarchy
- Republic
- Communist/Socialist state
- Federal republic

**Communism:** A system based on the 19th-century political theories of Karl Marx. Marx advocated class war and a society in which all property is publicly owned. Communist states are usually one-party and dictatorial.

**Dictatorship:** Rule by one person, a group or a committee whose word is law. The term *dictator* originated in ancient Rome when the Roman Senate could appoint individuals as "dictators" in times of national emergency.

**Federalism:** A union of two or more self-governing states which agree to accept a single government's rule in certain matters. Countries that have federal systems include the U.S.A., Australia, Canada, and Switzerland.

**Monarchy:** Rule by a king, queen, emperor, or empress. A monarch once had supreme power, but today a constitutional monarch's power is usually limited to mainly ceremonial duties by their country's constitution.

**Oligarchy:** Government by a small ruling group. A republic, for example, would be an oligarchy if only a few people were entitled to vote. Oligarchies in ancient times included most Greek city-states, where only certain citizens could vote.

**Republic:** A state where power is held by elected representatives acting on behalf of the people who elected them. An elected president rather than a monarch is head of state and/or head of the government.

## GOVERNMENT SYSTEMS

Two important democratic government systems are represented in the diagram by those of the United States of America (a federal republic) and the United Kingdom (a parliamentary monarchy).

The British system, which has no written constitution, has evolved over centuries with parliament gradually asserting its power. The U.S. system is based on a written constitution, approved in 1789.

### UNITED KINGDOM

### THE CROWN

Monarch is head of state; the government acts on behalf of the crown. The monarch has no power, but is kept informed of government actions.

### UNITED STATES OF AMERICA

### PRESIDENT

Head of State with executive powers, also head of the armed forces. Elected for a four-year term. Has power to appoint officials and veto laws passed by Congress.

### PRIME MINISTER

Head of government, usually chosen from the ruling party. Appoints government ministers, including senior Cabinet ministers. No fixed term of office.

### LEGISLATURE

Congress has two Houses, the Senate and the House of Representatives. All members are elected for fixed terms. They can pass laws and overturn the president's vetoes.

### PARLIAMENT

Two Houses, the elected Commons (650 members) and the non-elected Lords (hereditary and life peers, some bishops and judges). A general election must be held every five years.

### JUDICIARY

The U.S. Supreme Court is the highest court in the nation. The president appoints judges, subject to Senate consent, to decide whether laws are constitutional.

### JUDICIARY

Judges in the House of Lords are the highest court in the U.K. The judiciary is independent of government. No British court can overrule a decision of parliament.

## LOCAL GOVERNMENT

National governments run national affairs: taxation, finance, defense, and foreign policy. Many countries also have state or provincial governments which have considerable powers. At local level, regional and city government is carried out by assemblies of elected members and by appointed full-time officials. The responsibilities of local government vary from country to country but often include such services as education, town planning, sanitation, parks and recreation areas, police, fire services, and roads. To pay for these services, local governments usually collect taxes, paid by taxpayers in addition to national taxes.

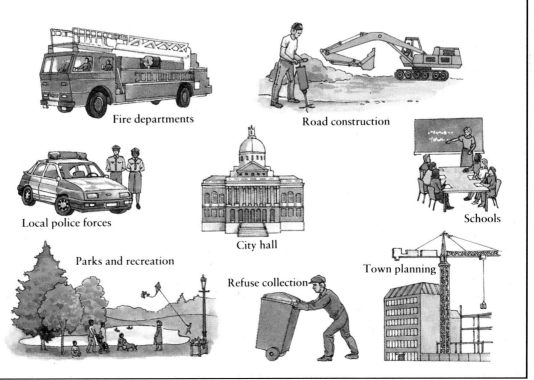

Fire departments

Road construction

Local police forces

Schools

City hall

Parks and recreation

Refuse collection

Town planning

# Government Facts and Records

The United Nations has more than 170 member countries. Each has its own system of government, often modeled on one of the major world systems (such as the U.S. or French presidential republics), but with their own distinctive characteristics. Monarchies survive in countries renowned for democratic liberalism, such as Sweden, as well as in more traditionally minded states, such as Saudi Arabia. Today, as throughout history, dictators rise and fall, usually setting their own records of misgovernment.

### FACTS ABOUT GOVERNMENT

- The only father and son to have served as U.S. presidents were the second, John Adams, and the sixth, John Quincy Adams. John Adams was the first president to live in the White House in Washington.
- As well as more than 170 self-governing countries, there are about 60 colonies or other territories ruled by larger nations.
- The first U.S. state or territory to give women the vote was the Territory of Wyoming, in 1869.
The first country to have universal suffrage was New Zealand, in 1893.
- The world's biggest democracy is India, with at least 500 million electors.
- The first woman to become prime minister was Sirimavo Bandaranaike of Ceylon (now Sri Lanka), in 1960.
- The only elected monarch in the world is the King of Malaysia.

▼ *The prophet of communism, Karl Marx (1818–1883), has had a greater influence on modern politics than any other person.*

## GOVERNMENT AND LAWMAKING

**National governments** make laws that apply throughout a nation. Countries (like Canada) are unions or federations, with power shared between the central government and regional governments which make their own laws.
**Laws** are proposed by the president, by government ministers, or by members of the lawmaking assembly. A law begins as a bill, which is discussed by the assembly, often altered, and then voted on before becoming law as an act.
The democratic idea of **one person, one vote** is a modern concept, dating from the 1800s.

▲ *Under the United Nations charter, the Security Council has responsibility for keeping world peace.*

▼ *The Capitol, in Washington, D.C., is the seat of the United States Congress.*

## VOTING

Before the 1800s few people had the right to vote, even in parliamentary systems. Black Americans had to struggle to win the vote and until the 1900s women took little part in government. Suffragette campaigns *(left)* won women the right to vote (1893 New Zealand, 1902 Australia, 1919 U.S.A., 1928 U.K.). Voting in some countries is not compulsory. In others (Australia, for example) everyone registered to vote in elections must do so.

▶ *The Vatican City State in Rome, headquarters of the government of the Roman Catholic Church, is the world's smallest self-governing state. It covers just 109 acres (44 hectares).*

## MONARCHY

Unlike other heads of state, monarchs usually inherit the throne from a member of their family such as their mother or father. In the past, monarchs often claimed that they were God's representatives; in Europe this belief was known as the "divine right of kings." The Japanese venerated their emperors as divine beings until 1946. After Japan's defeat in World War II, Emperor Hirohito renounced this ancient doctrine. Hirohito reigned as a constitutional monarch until his death in 1989, when his son Akihito succeeded him *(right)*.

# Conflict

People fought wars long before history first recorded the victors' triumphs. Territorial rivalry and the pursuit of power are common factors in most conflicts. The 20th century has seen two world wars and many smaller wars. The "cold war" between the U.S.S.R. and the U.S.A. ended in the early 1990s. The costly high-technology arms race between East and West has also stopped, but global peace remains an elusive goal. Terrorism and civil war still bring fear and devastation to the troublespots of the world.

▲ The Middle East has been a key area of 20th-century conflict. Saudi Arabians were in the allied force that fought Iraq in the 1991 Persian Gulf War.

**AREAS IN CONFLICT AROUND THE WORLD**

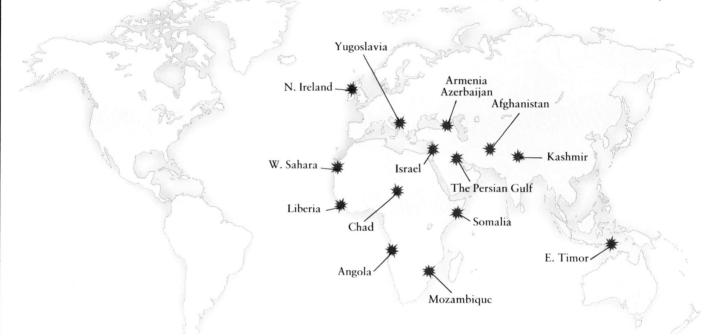

## SOME TROUBLESPOTS AROUND THE WORLD

**Afghanistan:** Soviet troops pulled out in 1989, but civil war continues between the government and guerrillas.

**Angola:** Civil war since 1970s between government and UNITA rebels.

**Armenia:** Newly independent ex-Soviet republic, fighting neighbor Azerbaijan over the disputed territory of Nagorno Karabakh.

**Chad:** Civil war, with Libya and France backing rival sides.

**East Timor:** Former Portuguese colony, ruled by Indonesia against the wishes of the local people.

**Israel:** At odds with its Arab neighbors since the foundation of a Jewish state in 1948.

**Kashmir:** Territory disputed between India and Pakistan.

**Liberia:** Civil war started in 1990 after rebels overthrew the president.

**Mozambique:** Civil war devastating the country and making five million people homeless.

**Northern Ireland:** A disputed part of U.K.; current terrorism began in the late 1960s.

**Persian Gulf:** Iraq invaded Kuwait 1990, defeated by Allied forces in 1991.

**Somalia:** Civil war following the collapse of the government of Siyad Barrah in 1991.

**Western Sahara:** Claimed by Morocco, a claim disputed by nationalist Polisario Front.

**Yugoslavia:** A former federal republic torn apart by civil war. Croatia, Slovenia, Bosnia-Herzegovina, and Macedonia are now independent.

▲ United Nations' soldiers in the former state of Yugoslavia in 1992. The UN lacks the military power to end conflicts but it can act as a peace-keeper between opposing sides.

◀ *The end of the Cold War saw the end of the Soviet Union's influence: here, in 1989, crowds in Prague's main square cheer Czechoslovak democracy leaders.*

▼ *Aircraft of the major powers: the Russian MiG-29 is an advanced fighter plane. The U.S. Air Force flies B-52 bombers, as well as the ultramodern Stealth.*

### THE COST OF A WORLD WAR

World War II (1939–1945) cost at least 55 million lives, more than all the previous wars in history put together. At least 40 million of those who died were civilians: the majority of them lived in Russia and Poland.

### ARMED FORCES DATAFILE

The U.S.A. has the world's most powerful armed forces, but relies on technology rather than mass manpower. The forces of the old Soviet Union, numerically the world's largest, are at present controlled by the republics of the Commonwealth of Independent States (C.I.S.). The graph *below* compares the world's five biggest armies.

#### LARGEST FIVE ARMIES

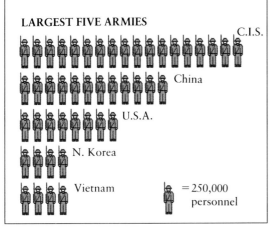

C.I.S.

China

U.S.A.

N. Korea

Vietnam

= 250,000 personnel

B-2 Stealth bomber

MiG-29

B-52

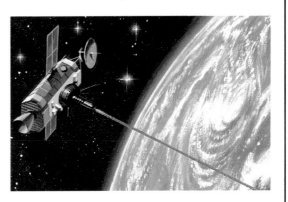

▶ *The U.S. Star Wars defense system uses computers, lasers, satellites, and missiles. It was originally designed to shoot down Soviet rockets. With the end of the Cold War, Russia and the U.S. may cooperate to create a defensive shield in space.*

▼ *The largest ships in the U.S. Navy, the world's biggest navy, are nuclear-powered aircraft carriers and three veteran battleships. Typhoon submarines (Russia) are the biggest in service.*

U.S.S. *Missouri*

U.S.S. *Nimitz*

Typhoon class submarine

# Flags

Not all flags are national flags. Rulers (presidents or queens, for example) may have their own flags. So, too, do organizations, such as the United Nations. Army regiments and ships have flags of their own, too. Some national flags have very long histories. Denmark, for instance, has had the same flag for more than 700 years. The Soviet Union's red flag of socialism, with its communist red star, hammer and sickle, has now given way to the various flags adopted or re-adopted by the independent republics.

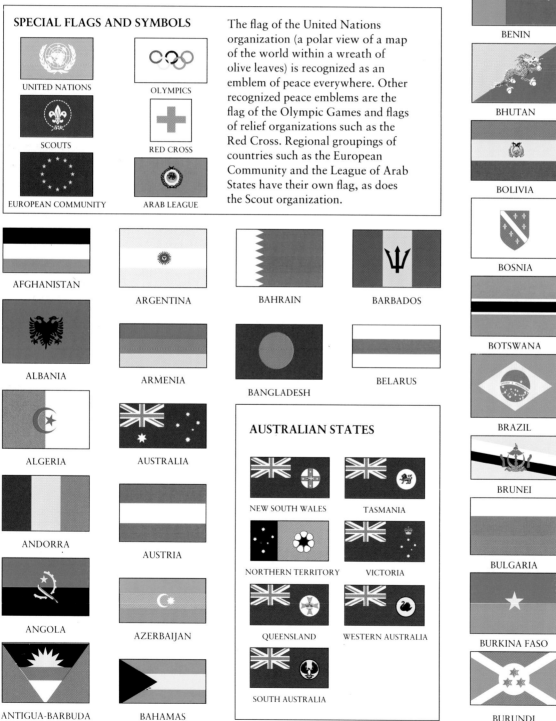

## SPECIAL FLAGS AND SYMBOLS

UNITED NATIONS

OLYMPICS

SCOUTS

RED CROSS

EUROPEAN COMMUNITY

ARAB LEAGUE

The flag of the United Nations organization (a polar view of a map of the world within a wreath of olive leaves) is recognized as an emblem of peace everywhere. Other recognized peace emblems are the flag of the Olympic Games and flags of relief organizations such as the Red Cross. Regional groupings of countries such as the European Community and the League of Arab States have their own flag, as does the Scout organization.

AFGHANISTAN

ARGENTINA

BAHRAIN

BARBADOS

ALBANIA

ARMENIA

BANGLADESH

BELARUS

ALGERIA

AUSTRALIA

## AUSTRALIAN STATES

ANDORRA

AUSTRIA

NEW SOUTH WALES

TASMANIA

ANGOLA

AZERBAIJAN

NORTHERN TERRITORY

VICTORIA

QUEENSLAND

WESTERN AUSTRALIA

ANTIGUA-BARBUDA

BAHAMAS

SOUTH AUSTRALIA

BELGIUM

CAMBODIA

BELIZE

CAMEROON

BENIN

CANADA

BHUTAN

CAPE VERDE

BOLIVIA

CENT AFRICAN REP

BOSNIA

CHAD

BOTSWANA

CHILE

BRAZIL

CHINA

BRUNEI

COLOMBIA

BULGARIA

COMOROS

BURKINA FASO

CONGO

BURUNDI

COSTA RICA

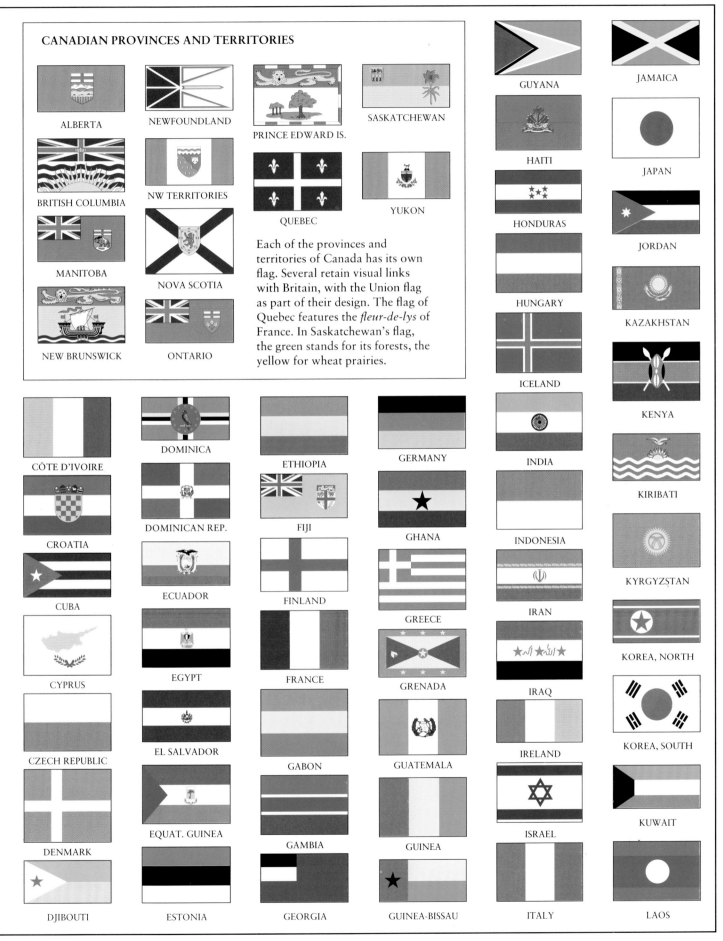

## CANADIAN PROVINCES AND TERRITORIES

ALBERTA

NEWFOUNDLAND

PRINCE EDWARD IS.

SASKATCHEWAN

BRITISH COLUMBIA

NW TERRITORIES

QUEBEC

YUKON

MANITOBA

NOVA SCOTIA

NEW BRUNSWICK

ONTARIO

Each of the provinces and territories of Canada has its own flag. Several retain visual links with Britain, with the Union flag as part of their design. The flag of Quebec features the *fleur-de-lys* of France. In Saskatchewan's flag, the green stands for its forests, the yellow for wheat prairies.

CÔTE D'IVOIRE

DOMINICA

ETHIOPIA

GERMANY

GUYANA

JAMAICA

CROATIA

DOMINICAN REP.

FIJI

GHANA

HAITI

JAPAN

CUBA

ECUADOR

FINLAND

GREECE

HONDURAS

JORDAN

CYPRUS

EGYPT

FRANCE

GRENADA

HUNGARY

KAZAKHSTAN

CZECH REPUBLIC

EL SALVADOR

GABON

GUATEMALA

ICELAND

KENYA

DENMARK

EQUAT. GUINEA

GAMBIA

GUINEA

INDIA

KIRIBATI

DJIBOUTI

ESTONIA

GEORGIA

GUINEA-BISSAU

INDONESIA

KYRGYZSTAN

IRAN

IRAQ

IRELAND

ISRAEL

ITALY

KOREA, NORTH

KOREA, SOUTH

KUWAIT

LAOS

81

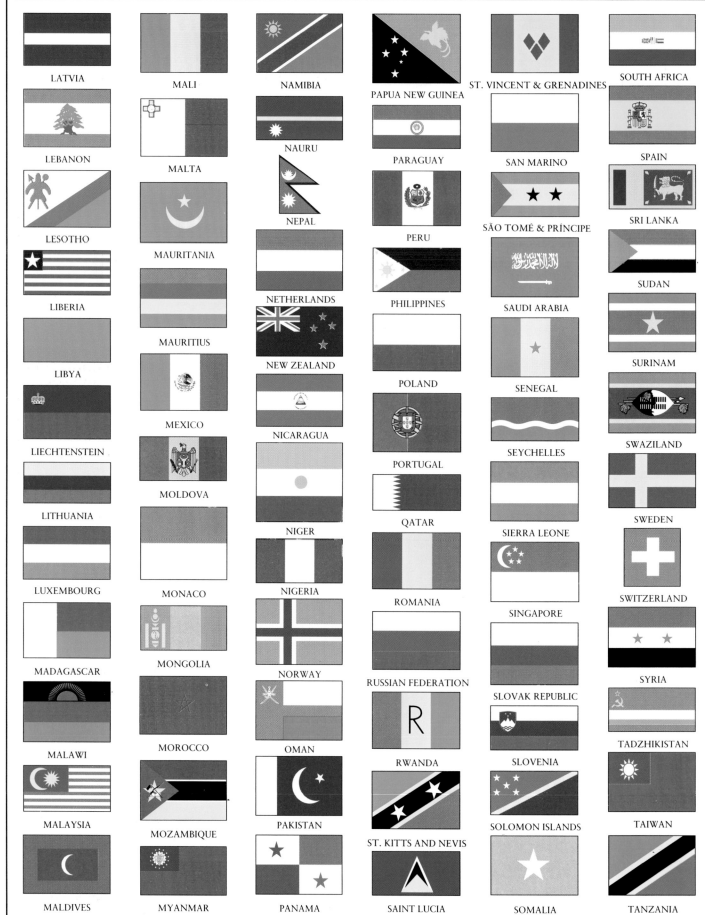

LATVIA

MALI

NAMIBIA

PAPUA NEW GUINEA

ST. VINCENT & GRENADINES

SOUTH AFRICA

LEBANON

MALTA

NAURU

PARAGUAY

SAN MARINO

SPAIN

LESOTHO

MAURITANIA

NEPAL

PERU

SÃO TOMÉ & PRÍNCIPE

SRI LANKA

LIBERIA

MAURITIUS

NETHERLANDS

PHILIPPINES

SAUDI ARABIA

SUDAN

LIBYA

MEXICO

NEW ZEALAND

POLAND

SENEGAL

SURINAM

LIECHTENSTEIN

MOLDOVA

NICARAGUA

PORTUGAL

SEYCHELLES

SWAZILAND

LITHUANIA

NIGER

QATAR

SIERRA LEONE

SWEDEN

LUXEMBOURG

MONACO

NIGERIA

ROMANIA

SINGAPORE

SWITZERLAND

MADAGASCAR

MONGOLIA

NORWAY

RUSSIAN FEDERATION

SLOVAK REPUBLIC

SYRIA

MALAWI

MOROCCO

OMAN

RWANDA

SLOVENIA

TADZHIKISTAN

MALAYSIA

MOZAMBIQUE

PAKISTAN

ST. KITTS AND NEVIS

SOLOMON ISLANDS

TAIWAN

MALDIVES

MYANMAR

PANAMA

SAINT LUCIA

SOMALIA

TANZANIA

# FLAGS OF THE U.S. STATES AND TERRITORIES

ALABAMA

DELAWARE

IOWA

MICHIGAN

NEW HAMPSHIRE

OKLAHOMA

TEXAS

WASHINGTON

ALASKA

FLORIDA

KANSAS

MINNESOTA

NEW JERSEY

OREGON

UTAH

WEST VIRGINIA

ARIZONA

GEORGIA

KENTUCKY

MISSISSIPPI

NEW MEXICO

PENNSYLVANIA

VERMONT

WISCONSIN

ARKANSAS

HAWAII

LOUISIANA

MISSOURI

NEW YORK

VIRGINIA

WYOMING

CALIFORNIA

IDAHO

MAINE

MONTANA

NTH CAROLINA

RHODE ISLAND

COLORADO

ILLINOIS

MARYLAND

NEBRASKA

STH CAROLINA

CONNECTICUT

INDIANA

MASSACHUSETTS

NEVADA

NTH DAKOTA

STH DAKOTA

OHIO

TENNESSEE

U.S. state and territory flags fall into five categories: those dating from the Revolutionary War (New York); those based on flags of the Confederacy (Florida); those used before joining the Union or from countries to which they once belonged (Utah); those derived from militia colors (Ohio), and those from competitions (Alaska).

THAILAND

TONGA

TUVALU

UNITED STATES

VENEZUELA

ZAIRE

TOGO

TRINIDAD & TOBAGO

UGANDA

URUGUAY

VIETNAM

ZAMBIA

## U.K. COUNTRIES

ENGLAND

SCOTLAND

WALES

TUNISIA

TURKEY

TURKMENISTAN

UKRAINE

UTD ARAB EMIRATES

UNITED KINGDOM

UZBEKISTAN

VANUATU

VATICAN CITY

WESTERN SAMOA

YEMEN

YUGOSLAVIA

ZIMBABWE

Flags authenticated by the Flag Research Center, Winchester, Mass. 01890 U.S.A.

All the flags shown are national flags as recognized by the United Nations.

# GLOSSARY

Words in **bold** indicate an entry elsewhere in the **Glossary** or **Gazetteer**

**Aborigines:** The original inhabitants of **Australia**.

**ASEAN:** Association of Southeast Asian Nations, founded 1967. Members are Brunei, **Indonesia, Malaysia, Philippines, Singapore,** and **Thailand**.

**Autocracy:** Government by one person, an absolute ruler or **dictator**.

**Balance of Trade:** Difference between a country's exports and imports.

**Benelux:** Economic union formed in 1948 by **Belgium, the Netherlands,** and Luxembourg.

**Berlin Wall:** Barricade in **Berlin, Germany,** built in 1961 by the East German communist government to prevent its citizens fleeing to the West. The Wall was opened up in November 1989, after the collapse of communism in East Germany.

**Boom:** Period of increased business activity; the opposite of a **slump**.

**Bundestag:** **Germany's** parliament.

**CACM:** Central American Common Market, founded 1960.

**Capital:** Money or property owned by a person or organization.

**Caricom:** Caribbean Community and Common Market, founded 1973. Members include most Caribbean island states, but not Cuba.

**Cash crop:** Crop grown for sale, often for export, rather than for the farmer's own use.

**Civil rights:** Freedoms that people ought to enjoy, such as freedom of speech or worship, or the right not to be imprisoned without cause.

**Civil war:** War fought between different groups living in the same country.

**Cold War:** Mutual suspicion between communist and non-communist countries following World War II. It was at its height in the 1950s when the **U.S.A.** and **U.S.S.R.** built up huge forces, including nuclear bombs and missiles; ended by the 1990s.

**Colony:** Territory fully or partly governed by a mother country.

**Command economy:** Economic system in which agriculture, trade, and industry are directed from central government—as in the old **U.S.S.R.** under communism.

**Commodity:** Anything that is produced for sale.

**Common market:** Group of countries who have formed an economic alliance, to encourage **free trade** between them.

**Commons, House of:** Lawmaking body of British parliament, to which Members of Parliament (MPs) are democratically elected.

**Commonwealth:** Loose association of former British-ruled states, dating from 1949 but with its origins in the earlier British Empire. Heads of government meet every two years. The British monarch is the symbolic head of the Commonwealth. Its most recent member is **Namibia**.

**Commonwealth of Independent States (C.I.S.):** Formed in 1991 as an attempt to preserve a loosely unified association of independent ex-Soviet republics, following the breakup of the **Soviet Union**.

**Congress:** **U.S.** lawmaking assembly or legislature, consisting of the House of Representatives and the Senate.

**Cortes:** **Spain's** parliament.

**Currency:** A country's money; examples are the German mark, British pound, French franc, and U.S. dollar.

**Customs duty:** Tax paid on **imports** or **exports**.

**Dail:** **Ireland's** parliament.

**Debt:** Money owed by a person, a business or a country.

**Dependent territory:** One governed by another, for example a **colony**.

**Detente:** Easing of political tension or disagreement between countries.

**Developing nation:** A poor country that is building up its industries and modernizing its agriculture.

**Dictator:** Ruler with total authority over a country; a position often obtained by overthrowing the lawful authorities.

**European Community (EC):** Free trade and customs union originally set up by the ECSC Treaty of 1952. Its original members were **Belgium, France, West Germany, Italy,** Luxembourg, and the **Netherlands**. By 1992 the EC was 12-strong (including the **U.K.,** Denmark, **Ireland, Greece, Spain,** and **Portugal**) and was expanding into an economic and political union.

**ECOWAS:** Economic Community of West African States, founded 1975, with its headquarters in **Nigeria**.

**EFTA:** European Free Trade Association, formed 1960 (**Austria, Iceland, Norway, Sweden, Finland,** and **Switzerland**). Entered into free trade agreements with **EC** in 1973.

**Excise duty:** Tax on goods produced or sold within the country of origin.

**Exports:** Goods a country sells to other countries.

**FAO:** Food and Agriculture Organization of the **United Nations**.

**Federation:** Group of states with some self-government but with some matters (such as defense) governed by a central authority.

**Fertilizers:** Substances added to soil to boost crop yields, can be artificial chemicals or natural (such as manure).

**Fossil fuels:** Hydrocarbon fuels such as petroleum, gas, and coal. This resource will eventually run out.

**Free trade area:** An area covered by an agreement between certain countries to remove tariffs and other barriers to international trade.

**G7 States:** Informal group of seven leading Western nations: **Canada, France, Germany, Japan, Italy, United Kingdom,** and the **United States**.

**GATT:** General Agreement on Tariffs and Trade, a treaty (1948) signed by about 100 countries, to promote trade between those countries.

**Gross domestic product:** Means of measuring a country's economic strength; the sum of all output (money spent, goods sold, income earned) in one year.

**Gross national product:** GNP is gross domestic product plus all income a country receives from abroad.

**Guerrilla:** Irregular (i.e. non-army) soldier, usually fighting in a rebellion or **civil war**.

**Gulf Cooperation Council:** Set up in 1981 by Arab states in the Persian Gulf.

**IMF:** International Monetary Fund, a **United Nations** agency.

**Imports:** Goods a country buys from other countries.

**Interest:** Price paid for use of someone else's money.

**International Court of Justice:** A **United Nations** court of 15 elected judges, that meets at The Hague, in the Netherlands.

**Kurds:** A Middle Eastern people with no

84

national territory of their own. Kurds live in **Turkey** and **Iraq**, and the plight of Iraqi Kurds during and after the **Persian Gulf War** of 1991 brought their problems to worldwide notice.

**Labor**: Means work, but is used also to describe people who work for wages in factories, farms, offices, etc.

**LAIA**: Latin American Integration Association (also known as ALADI), a free trade community set up in 1980 by countries of South America.

**League of Arab States**: Known as The Arab League, founded in 1945 by Arab countries to foster cultural and economic ties among Arab states. It also represents member states in some international negotiations.

**Market economy**: System in which individuals and businesses control investment and production.

**Mint**: Government-run factory for making banknotes and coins.

**Monarch**: Hereditary ruler, such as a king, queen, or emperor.

**Nationalism**: Belief in the idea that a national identity should be preserved.

**NATO**: North Atlantic Treaty Organization, a military alliance founded (1949) by Western nations to defend Europe and the North Atlantic Ocean from military aggression by the **Soviet Union**.

**OAS**: Organization of American States (nations), founded in 1948, with headquarters in **Washington, D.C. Cuba** was excluded from OAS activities in 1962.

**OAU** Organization of African Unity, founded (1963) to promote African unity and cooperation; by 1991 it had a membership of 50 countries. The headquarters are in Addis Ababa, Ethiopia.

**OECD**: Organization for Economic Cooperation and Development, founded (1961) to promote social and economic welfare in member countries. Headquarters in **Paris, France**. Members include most Western European states, **Japan, Australia, Canada**, and the **U.S.A.**

**OPEC** Organization of Petroleum Exporting Countries, founded (1960) by oil-producing states to coordinate oil production and prices.

**Patron saint**: Christian saint believed by faithful to have special care for certain things: for example, St.

Christopher is the patron saint of travelers, St. Patrick the patron saint of **Ireland**.

**Persian Gulf War**: Fought in 1991 between **Iraq** and **UN**-backed international coalition of forces (including U.S., Canadian, British, French, Arab), following Iraq's invasion of **Kuwait** in 1990. Iraq withdrew from Kuwait and suffered considerable losses.

**President**: Elected (usually) head of state or government in a republic.

**Private enterprise** *see* **Market economy**

**Product**: Anything that is made.

**Racism**: Dislike, unfair treatment, and persecution of one people by another on account of their race.

**Referendum**: National vote on a particular issue.

**Refugee**: Someone forced to flee their home by war or natural disaster.

**Sanctions**: Withholding goods or services as a punishment or as a means of persuasion. In recent years UN sanctions have been enforced against **Iraq** and **South Africa**, banning trade in certain goods with those countries.

**Sect**: In religion, a group of people within one faith but with their own separate beliefs and practices.

**Security Council**: 15-strong UN body concerned with maintaining peace and security between countries. The five permanent members are **China, France, Russia, U.K.,** and the **U.S.A.**; the other ten members are elected for two-year terms.

**Slump**: Decline in trade and industry, causing business closures and unemployment.

**Solar energy**: Power derived from sunlight, for example, through heating panels in house roofs.

**South Pacific**: Forum founded in 1971 to further cooperation between Pacific nations, including **Australia, New Zealand**, Papua New Guinea, and other island states.

**Soviet Union**: The former Union of Soviet Socialist Republics (U.S.S.R.); many of the former republics of the U.S.S.R. are now independent countries of the **C.I.S.**

**Star Wars**: Popular name for U.S. Strategic Defense Initiative, a defensive anti-missile system. Work on developing the hugely costly system began in the 1980s but was

slowed when relations between **U.S.A.** and **Soviet Union** improved.

**START**: Strategic Arms Reduction Treaty, signed in 1990 by **U.S.A.** and **U.S.S.R.** and agreeing to cut their missile forces.

**Subsistence farmers**: Farmers who grow only enough food to feed their own families but have no surplus to sell.

**Superpower**: Countries such as the **U.S.A.** and the former **Soviet Union** that have the power to dominate world politics.

**Third World, The**: Term used to describe developing countries of Africa, Asia, and Latin America; originally, those countries which did not support either the West or the **Soviet Union** during the **Cold War**.

**Tidal power**: Harnessing the ocean tides in a barrage or a dam to drive generators to make electricity.

**Treaty**: Written agreement between two or more nations.

**United Nations (UN)**: An international organization, formed (1945) to promote world peace. By 1991 it had 166 member nations; its headquarters are in **New York City**.

**UN Secretary-General**: Chief administrative officer of the **United Nations**.

**UNESCO**: The United Nations Educational, Scientific and Cultural Organization is an agency of the **UN** set up to promote the exchange of information, ideas, and culture. Its headquarters are in **Paris**.

**UNICEF**: The United Nations Children's Fund was set up by the **UN** to assist governments meet the long-term needs of child welfare. Its headquarters are in **New York City**.

**Wall Street**: Located in Manhattan, **New York City**, a street that includes the New York Stock Exchange and many other financial institutions. Its name is often used in general reference to American money markets.

**Warsaw Pact**: Former military alliance (1955) of European communist countries, under the leadership of the **Soviet Union**. It was dissolved in 1991.

**WHO**: World Health Organization, a **UN** agency concerned with fighting disease and improving health standards.

# GAZETTEER

**Afghanistan:** Republic in southwest Asia; has experienced long civil war between government and Islamic fundamentalist guerrillas, and invasion by Soviet troops (1979–1989).

**Albania:** Small country in southeast Europe; a communist state after World War II until the early 1990s.

**Amazon:** The most important river in South America. Second longest river in the world, 4,000 miles (6,448 km).

**Amsterdam:** Capital of the Netherlands.

**Angel Falls, Venezuela:** Highest waterfall in the world, 3,212 ft. (978 m).

**Arabia:** Peninsula in southwest Asia, the Arabian Desert is the third biggest in the world.

**Argentina:** Republic in southern South America; a Spanish colony until 1816. Went to war with Britain in 1982 over its longstanding claim to the **Falkland Islands**.

**Athens:** Capital of **Greece**.

**Australia:** Continent and largest island country in the Pacific Ocean; at first a British colony, in 1901 it became an independent federation of States.

**Australian Desert:** Several deserts combining to form the world's second largest desert region.

**Austria:** Republic in central Europe.

**Balearic Islands:** A group of Mediterranean islands that includes Majorca, Minorca, and Ibiza; a province of **Spain**.

**Balkans:** Mountainous peninsula in southeast Europe.

**Baltic States:** Former Soviet republics of Estonia, Latvia, and Lithuania.

**Bangladesh:** Country of the Indian subcontinent. It formed part of **India** from 1857 until 1947 when it became known as East **Pakistan**; it became an independent republic in 1971.

**Beijing (Peking):** Capital of **China**.

**Belgium:** Country in western Europe; people speak both Flemish (a Dutch dialect) and French.

**Berlin:** Capital of **Germany**.

**Bolivia:** Land-locked country in central South America; a Spanish colony until 1825.

**Borneo:** A large island in Asia, that includes Brunei and parts of **Malaysia** and **Indonesia**; the third biggest island in the world.

**Bosnia-Herzegovina:** Former Yugoslav republic, now an independent state.

**Brazil:** The largest country in South America and the world's fifth largest nation; Portuguese colony until 1826.

**Brittany:** Westernmost region of **France**, forming a peninsula between the Bay of Biscay and the English Channel.

**Brussels:** Capital of **Belgium** and headquarters of the EC.

**Bucharest:** Capital of **Romania**.

**Budapest:** Capital of **Hungary**.

**Bulgaria:** Country in southwest Europe; until the collapse of the U.S.S.R. in 1989 Bulgaria was a communist state.

**Burma** *see* **Myanmar**

**Cairo:** Capital of **Egypt**.

**Calcutta:** Largest city in **India**.

**California:** U.S. state with the most people (about 30 million).

**Cambodia (Kampuchea 1976–1989):** Country in Southeast Asia recovering from a civil war (1970–1975), in which millions of its people died.

**Canada:** World's second-largest nation after Russia; covers entire northern part of North America excepting Alaska but with less than seven people per square mile.

**Canary Islands:** A group of islands in the Atlantic Ocean that belong to **Spain**.

**Canberra:** Capital of **Australia**.

**Cape Town:** Important port and legislative capital of South Africa.

**Caspian Sea:** The world's largest lake, 143,244 sq. miles (371,000 sq. km); situated in Asia.

**Channel Islands:** Islands geographically close to France but part of the U.K.

**Chicago:** Third-largest U.S. city, situated on Lake Michigan, Illinois.

**Chile:** Country that extends down the west of southern South America; a Spanish colony until 1818.

**China:** World's third biggest country by area and the largest by population; ruled by communists since 1949.

**Colombia:** Country in northwest of South America; a Spanish colony until the early 1800s.

**Croatia:** Former Yugoslav republic, now independent.

**Cyprus:** Large island in the Mediterranean Sea, with population of mainly Greek and Turkish origin; a republic since 1960, the northern part of the island has been occupied by **Turkey** since 1974.

**Czechoslovakia:** Country in eastern Europe which threw off communist rule in 1989. In 1990 name changed to Czech and Slovak Federal Republic and discussions began over the eventual splitting of the country into two independent countries.

**Danube:** River in Europe, rises in **Germany**, flows east into Black Sea for 1,771 miles (2,850 km).

**Denmark:** Monarchy in northern Europe; most southerly part of **Scandinavia**.

**Dublin:** Capital of the Republic of **Ireland**.

**Ecuador:** Country situated on the Equator in northwest South America; a Spanish colony until 1822.

**Egypt:** Arab republic in northeast Africa; in the 1980s and 1990s a leader in the peace process to end the hostility between the Arab states and **Israel**.

**Elbrus:** Mountain in Caucasus Mountains, Europe's highest peak, 18,480 ft. (5,633 m).

**Eritrea:** Part of Ethiopia in northeast Africa, whose people are fighting for independence.

**Everest:** World's highest mountain, 29,028 ft. (8,848 m); situated in the Himalayas on the border of Tibet and Nepal.

**Falkland Islands:** Group of islands in the South Atlantic, a colony of the U.K. since 1833. British sovereignty has long been disputed by **Argentina**, which led to brief Argentinian occupation in 1982.

**Finland:** Country in northeast Europe; declared independence from **Russia** in 1917 and has remained neutral since World War II.

**France:** Large country in western Europe; one of Europe's wealthiest and most powerful nations.

**Ganges:** River in northern **India**, sacred to Hindus.

**Germany:** Europe's most successful industrial nation, reunited in 1990 after being divided into two countries (East and West Germany) since the end of World War II in 1945.

**Gibraltar:** Rocky headland on the southern tip of **Spain**; a British colony since 1713.

**Gobi:** Desert in **Mongolia** and **China**; the fourth biggest desert in the world.

**Grand Canyon, Arizona:** The world's longest inland gorge, formed by the Colorado River.

**Greece:** Country in southeast Europe, comprising a peninsula and many islands; a republic since 1973.

**Greenland:** Self-governing part of **Denmark** and the world's largest island (excluding Australia).

**Himalayas:** The great mountain range in Asia that stretches for over 1,600 miles (2,600 km) and includes the world's highest peaks. *See* **Everest**

**Hiroshima:** City in **Japan** destroyed in 1945 during World War II by the first atomic bomb.

**Hokkaido:** Most northerly of the four main islands of **Japan**.

**Hong Kong:** British colony on southeast coast of **China**, due to be returned to China in 1997.

**Honshu:** Largest main island of **Japan**.

**Hungary:** Country in central Europe; under the influence of the Soviet Union since the end of World War II, Hungary abandoned communism for a democratic government in 1989.

**Iberian Peninsula:** the name for the southwest peninsula of Europe comprising **Spain** and **Portugal**.

**Iceland:** Island in North Atlantic; a Scandinavian country, it has been an independent republic since 1944.

**India:** The world and Asia's second largest country by population, and the world's largest democracy.

**Indonesia:** Large island group in south-east Asia; main islands include Java, Sumatra, South Borneo, and West New Guinea (Irian Jaya).

**Iran:** Islamic republic in the **Middle East**. Iran was led by the Ayatollah Khomeini after the fall of the Shah in 1979; fought war with neighboring **Iraq** (1980–1988).

**Iraq:** Islamic republic in the **Middle East**; a kingdom (under British administration) until 1958. Under President Saddam Hussein, Iraq was at war with **Iran** (1980–1988). After its invasion of **Kuwait** (1990), Iraq then fought an international coalition force in the **Persian Gulf War** of 1991.

**Ireland:** The Republic of Ireland occupies four-fifths of an island situated west of Great Britain; an independent state since 1921.

**Israel:** Jewish state in what was formerly British-ruled Palestine. Israel was founded in 1948, since when it has fought four wars with its hostile Arab neighbors. It is the most highly industrialized country in the **Middle East**, especially for textiles.

**Italy:** Country in southern Europe; a republic since 1946.

**Japan:** Country in eastern Asia; it is the leading economic power in the region and the world's most successful trading nation.

**Java:** Most populated island of **Indonesia**, with 60 percent of the country's people.

**Jordan:** Arab kingdom in **Middle East**.

**Kenya:** Republic in East Africa; one of Africa's most prosperous nations.

**Kilimanjaro, Tanzania:** Highest mountain in Africa, 19,340 ft. (5,895 m).

**Korea, North and South:** Country of eastern Asia. Separate republics were declared in 1948. In the Korean War (1950–1953), the UN supported South Korea and communist China supported North Korea.

**Kuwait:** Oil rich emirate in the **Middle East**; invaded by **Iraq** in 1990 and freed by an international coalition after the **Persian Gulf War** of 1991.

**Kyushu:** Most southerly of the main islands of **Japan**.

**Lapland:** The most northerly region of **Scandinavia**; inhabited by Lapps.

**Lake Superior:** Largest lake in North America, 31,700 sq. miles (82,103 sq. km).

**Lake Victoria:** Largest lake in Africa, 26,834 sq. miles (69,500 sq. km).

**Lebanon:** Country in the **Middle East**; a prosperous trading center for the region; a long civil war in the 1970s and 1980s made it one of the world's most troubled countries.

**Libya:** Oil-rich republic in North Africa; Libya has often had difficult relationships with other countries during the 1950s to 1990s.

**London:** Capital of the United Kingdom.

**Los Angeles:** Second largest city in the U.S.; Hollywood, center of the American movie industry, is a suburb.

**Macedonia:** Small republic of former Yugoslavia seeking independence; also a region of **Greece**.

**Madagascar:** Country situated off the east coast of Africa, the fourth biggest island in the world.

**Madrid:** Capital of **Spain**.

**Malaysia:** Country comprising a federation of states in Southeast Asia.

**Marseille:** Important Mediterranean port in southern **France**.

**Mexico:** Country in Central America; was under Spanish rule until 1821.

**Mexico City:** Capital of **Mexico** and the world's second most populous city.

**Middle East:** Region that includes countries between the Near and Far East from **Egypt** in Africa to **Iran** in southwest Asia.

**Mississippi:** Longest river in North America, about 2,350 miles (3,780 km).

**Mont Blanc, France/Italy:** Highest mountain in western Europe 15,770 ft. (4,807 m).

**Montreal:** City in Quebec, **Canada**; the largest city in Canada; also the largest French-speaking city outside France.

**Moscow:** Capital of **Russia**.

**Mount McKinley, Alaska:** Highest mountain in North America, 20,320 ft. (6,194 m).

**Mount St. Helens:** Volcano in Washington State; erupted 1980 after being dormant since 1857.

**Mozambique:** Country on the east coast of Africa, formerly a Portuguese colony; has suffered from civil war since the 1980s.

**Myanmar:** Formerly Burma, country in Southeast Asia which has had a harsh military government since the 1960s and little contact with the outside world since.

**Namibia:** Country in southwest Africa, ruled by **South Africa** (against UN wishes) until 1990.

**Netherlands:** Country (often called **Holland**) in western Europe.

**New Guinea:** Largest island in the Pacific Ocean and second largest island in the world; politically divided into Irian Jaya (an **Indonesian** province) in the western half, **Papua New Guinea** in the eastern half.

**New York City:** Biggest city and the greatest port in the U.S.A.; the island of Manhattan is the city's cultural and commercial center.

**New Zealand:** Country in South Pacific consisting of North and South Islands and a number of smaller islands; a former British colony, it gained full independence in 1931.

**Niagara:** Twin falls in North America between **Canada** and the **U.S.A.**, maximum 160 ft. high, 2,500 ft. wide (50 m high, 760 m wide) on Canadian side.

**Nicaragua**: Largest country in Central America; a republic since 1838, the country was torn by revolution during the 1970s and 1980s.

**Nigeria**: Country in West Africa. Under British influence in 18th and 19th century, independent since 1960; Africa's most populous country.

**Nile**: Longest river in the world, 4,160 miles (6,670 km).

**Norway**: Monarchy occupying northern and western part of **Scandinavia**.

**Ottawa**: Capital of Canada.

**Pakistan**: Country in southern Asia; part of **India** until 1947, when it became an independent Islamic state. In 1971 East Pakistan became **Bangladesh**.

**Paraguay**: Landlocked country in central South America; gained independence from **Spain** in 1811.

**Paris**: Capital of **France**.

**Patagonia**: Cool, dry plateau at tip of South America; region is part of both southern **Argentina** and **Chile**.

**Philippines**: Republic in Southeast Asia, consisting of more than 7,000 islands.

**Poland**: Country in eastern Europe; under influence of U.S.S.R. since the end of World War II, Poland abandoned communism in the late 1980s.

**Portugal**: Country in southwest Europe; a republic, Portugal occupies the western part of the Iberian Peninsula.

**Pyrenees**: Range of mountains separating **France** and **Spain**.

**Quebec**: French-speaking province of **Canada**.

**Rhine**: Important river in western Europe, 820 miles (1,320 km), flowing from **Switzerland** through **Germany** and reaching the North Sea through the **Netherlands**.

**Romania**: Country in southeast Europe; after World War II Romania became a communist state, until the fall (1989) of the communist dictator Ceaucescu.

**Rome**: Capital of **Italy**.

**Rotterdam**: The Netherlands' and Europe's biggest port.

**Russia**: Largest of the republics making up the old Soviet Union, an independent country since 1991.

**Sahara**: Biggest desert in the world, covering much of northern Africa.

**St. Petersburg**: Formerly Leningrad (1924–1991), second city and former capital of **Russia**.

**San Marino**: World's smallest independent republic; it claims to be Europe's oldest independent state (from 4th century A.D.).

**Sardinia**: Large island in the Mediterranean Sea, part of **Italy**.

**Saudi Arabia**: Oil-rich, conservatively ruled kingdom in southwest Asia, occupying most of Arabian Peninsula.

**Serbia**: Dominant (by population) republic of former Yugoslavia.

**Sicily**: Large island in the Mediterranean Sea, part of **Italy**.

**Singapore**: Prosperous small republic off the southern tip of Malay Peninsula in Southeast Asia; consists of island of Singapore and over 50 smaller islands.

**Slovenia**: Former Yugoslav republic, now independent.

**Somalia (Somali Republic)**: Country in northeast Africa, torn by civil war since 1988.

**South Africa**: Republic in southern Africa. Until reforms began in late 1980s, the majority black population had few rights, and were ruled by a white minority government which enforced a system of *apartheid* (separation of the races).

**Spain**: Country in southwest Europe occupying most of the Iberian Peninsula. Spain became a monarchy in 1975; it was a republic (1931–1939) and a dictatorship under Franco (1939–1975).

**Sri Lanka**: Island off coast of **India** in southern Asia (formerly Ceylon); independent since 1972.

**Stockholm**: Capital of **Sweden**.

**Sudan**: Largest country in Africa; independent since 1956, it has suffered from prolonged civil war.

**Sweden**: Monarchy that occupies northeastern part of **Scandinavia**.

**Switzerland**: Prosperous small country in central Europe; divided into French, German, and Italian-speaking areas, it was neutral in both world wars.

**Sydney**: Largest city and most important port in **Australia**.

**Syria**: Country in **Middle East**; an Arab republic since 1941.

**Taiwan (Nationalist China)**: Island republic, formerly Formosa, off the coast of **China**.

**Thailand**: Country in Southest Asia (known as Siam until 1939).

**Tokyo**: Capital of **Japan** and the world's biggest city.

**Toronto**: Largest city in **Canada**.

**Turkey**: Republic in southwest Asia with a small region in southeast Europe.

**Ukraine**: Independent country on the borders of Europe and Asia; until 1990 a republic of the U.S.S.R.

**United Kingdom**: Kingdom of Great Britain (England, Scotland, and Wales) and N. Ireland (since 1922).

**United States of America**: Country occupying most of southern part of N. America; the world's fourth largest country, it includes 50 states and the Federal District of Columbia. Since World War II it has been the world's leading economic and military power.

**Uruguay**: Country in South America; a former Spanish colony that won its independence in 1825.

**Vatican City**: Independent papal state in **Rome**; seat of government of Roman Catholic Church.

**Venezuela**: Country in northern South America; onetime Spanish colony became fully independent in 1830.

**Vienna**: Capital of **Austria**.

**Vietnam**: Republic in Southeast Asia, the setting for bitter fighting from 1946 (against French colonial rule) and from 1959 between South and North Vietnam. The U.S.A. became involved in the Vietnam War, which ended in 1975 with victory for the communist North, followed by reunification between the North and South.

**Volga**: Longest river in Europe, 2,194 miles (3,531 km).

**Washington, D.C.**: Capital of the **United States**; D.C. stands for District of Columbia.

**Wellington**: Capital of **New Zealand**.

**West Indies**: Group of islands off coast of N. and S. America that enclose the Caribbean Sea; they include Jamaica, Barbados, Cuba, and Puerto Rico.

**Yemen**: Islamic republic in southern Arabia, formed by unification of Yemen Arab Republic and People's Democratic Republic of Yemen (1990).

**Zaire**: Republic in central Africa, the second largest country in Africa.

**Zaire River (formerly the Congo)**: Second longest river in Africa, 2,900 miles (4,700 km).

**Zimbabwe**: Republic in southeast Africa; formerly the British colony of Rhodesia, independent since 1980.

# INDEX

The publishers would like to thank the following artists
for contributing to the book:

Marion Appleton 56–57, 58–59, 60, 76
Kuo Kang Chen 48–49, 51, 57, 67, 72–73, 79
Micheal Fisher (Garden Studio) 16–17, 26–27, 32–33, 38–39
41, 56–57, 76, 77
Eugene Fleury 10–11, 12–13, 14–15, 18–19, 22–23, 25, 28–29,
31, 34–35, 36–37, 40–41, 44, 46–47, 49, 50–51, 52, 62, 66,
69, 70
Chris Forsey 18, 20–21, 31, 42–43, 45, 71
Mark Franklin 74
Peter Jarvis 60
Deborah Kindred (Simon Girling and Associates) 65, 75
Malcolm Porter 48, 66–67, 68, 73
Michael Rotte 62–63, 69, 79
John Scorey 48, 53, 54–55, 58, 62–63, 64, 70–71, 74


The publishers wish to thank the following for supplying
photographs for this book:

Page 12 ZEFA; 16 *t* Spectrum, *b* ZEFA; 17 ZEFA; 18 *t* ZEFA, *c* ZEFA, *b* The Hutchison Library; 20 Grisewood
& Dempsey; 21 *c* Richard Powers/Trip *b* ZEFA; 23 ZEFA; 25 ZEFA; 26 Spectrum; 27 *c* ZEFA, *b* Spectrum; 28
ZEFA; 29 Robert Harding Picture Library; 31 ZEFA; 32 ZEFA; 34 *t* ZEFA, *b* Christine Osborne Pictures; 38
Robert Harding Picture Library; 39 ZEFA; 41 *t* ZEFA, *c* Spectrum; 42 ZEFA; 43 ZEFA; 45 *c* ZEFA, *b*
P.Gurling/British Antarctic Survey; 50 ZEFA; 51 Robert Harding Picture Library; 53 *t* Frank Spooner Pictures,
*b* Panos Pictures; 54 ZEFA; 58 *t* South American Pictures, *b* Frank Spooner Pictures; 59 The Hutchison Library;
60 Robert Harding Picture Library; 61 *t* Rex Features, *b* Edinburgh Festival Fringe; 62 ZEFA; 63 Spectrum; 65
Robert Harding Picture Library; 67 *t* ZEFA, *b* Robert Harding Picture Library; 68 Spectrum; 71 Spectrum; 72
Rex Features; 73 British Red Cross; 76 Rex Features; 77 *t* Mary Evans Picture Library, *b* Frank Spooner
Pictures;78 *t* Frank Spooner, *b* Rex Features; 79 Frank Spooner Pictures.

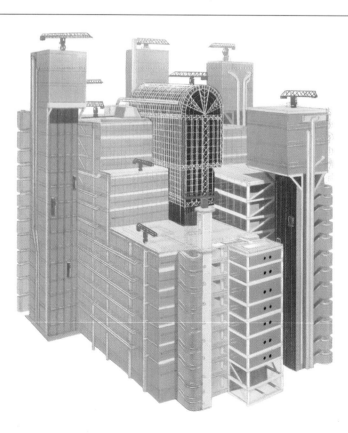